Colin Teevan

ŠVEJK

based on

The Good Soldier Švejk
and his Fortunes in the Great War

by

Jaroslav Hašek

OBERON BOOKS
LONDON

First published in 1999 by Oberon Books Ltd.

(incorporating Absolute Classics)

521 Caledonian Road, London N7 9RH

Tel: 0171 607 3637 / Fax: 0171 607 3629

e-mail: oberon.books@btinternet.com

A catalogue record for this book is available from the British Library.

ISBN 1 84002 119 5

Cover design: Andrzej Klimowski

Typography: Richard Doust

Printed in Great Britain by MPG Ltd., Bodmin.

ŠVEJK

for Madeline

Contents

INTRODUCTION

Jaroslav Hašek, son of a schoolteacher, was born in Prague in 1883 and died just short of forty years later in Lipnice in Bohemia. During his brief life, he met with a marked lack of success, in work, love or financial gain, only achieving recognition at the end of it with the publication of the one work by which he is internationally known today.

After his father died, when Hašek was thirteen, his work at school, until then promising, began to go to pieces. He became involved in street fights, and, after a number of complaints from the school and the police, he was expelled. His mother's efforts found him two jobs in chemists' shops, from the first of which he was dismissed for practical joking – accounts differ about what he did exactly – while he left the second on the recommendation of an understanding employer, who recognised the boy's gifts and persuaded his mother to send him to the Commercial Academy for further education. At the end of his time there, he decided to devote himself full-time to writing, making his first bow with a book of poems in 1903, which he followed up with a collection of five stories (1911) about *The Remarkable History of the Good Soldier Švejk* in which the dog-handler hero and resourceful sad sack makes his first appearance.

His collected journalism runs to some twelve hundred pieces, of varying types and certainly varying quality. His collected works were finally published in the late fifties, in nineteen volumes.

In the wake of wanderings in Central and Southern Europe, Hašek finished the First World War in Russia, as a prisoner, where he became a member of the Russian Communist Party, in which he was a Commissar, in Eastern Russia, for two years. Despite this practical service and his grotesque attacks on the military and social labyrinths of the dying Austro-Hungarian monarchy, it was not possible to pigeon-hole him in any recognisable category, being mainly driven by self-indulgence and an almost dedicated lack of principle. The only constant in his life and pursuits seemed to be drinking too much – certainly not the first journalist to do that. A firm anti-intellectual, he did not have very much time for the workers. He is said to have worked down the mines for a while, though it must have been a shortish while, and it is by no means certain what it was he was mining. A thorough-going Bohemian, by nature as well as nationality, he probably did well not to stay too long in any one place. Particularly, one guesses, post-revolutionary Russia, where veterans of the Fifth Army made formal objection to the libellous picture of military life in *Švejk*, accusing the author of having disparaged the spirit of idealism which informed the struggle for the liberation of Siberia. One might ask how idealistic the common Švejk-style soldiers were who bore the brunt of that struggle, but then, it is always dangerous to take on revolutionaries on the grounds of humour, a quality in which they seem frequently to have submitted to by-pass surgery.

It is, of course, with Švejk that we are mainly concerned. After his tentative first appearance in 1911, he blossomed after the war into the hero of a whole book, albeit an incomplete one. The first three parts of *The Adventures of the Good Soldier Švejk* came out in 1920-1923, in which later year Hašek died. A final part, *The Adventures of the Good Soldier in Russian Captivity*, significantly different in both style and concept, written by Karel Vaněk, appeared in 1923-24. How much of it was reliant on received ideas from Hašek is uncertain. For a long time, official Czech literary criticism looked down on *Švejk* as 'an abcess on the body of Czech literature'; it was indeed only the turnaround in Czech politics that allowed it to be admitted as a masterpiece, by which time it had been translated into eighteen languages, and had acquired such a high reputation abroad that it could hardly be denied an honoured position at home. The stylised vernacular of the novel, the expressivity of which rests on a sort of symbiosis of German and Czech, makes it a nightmare for translators, and more than usually difficult to achieve more than a limited approximation to the original. Nevertheless, limited or not, it has survived into eighteen languages, however unsatisfactorily.

Švejk has the quality of a folk-song or a well-remembered joke – who makes up jokes? who composes folk-songs? – in that one does not think of him as having been made up by Hašek or anyone else. He belongs, with Don Quixote and Gulliver, to the great company of satirical heroes of world literature, with the difference that he is unlike them in being genuinely stupid. A quality he defends jealously and heartily and with an unshakeable calm. The soldier, and everyone is afraid that that might be him at some time or other, has always two enemies — one is The Enemy and the other the system to which he is subordinated, the whole military apparatus which grinds him inexorably to powder between its wheels. Švejk's ability to deal with this, and it is not a conscious technique, but an inborn instinct for realism, is to do what he is told. He makes no effort to swim against the stream, with the result that he keeps his head above water. The 'good-ness' of the 'good soldier' is the despair of those surrounding him. Whatever happens to him, and there is a good deal that does, nothing can really *happen* to him. His obedience to the orders of his superiors – and who is not his superior? – is as dangerous a quality as rebellion. Ordered to fly an aeroplane he replies, 'Where to, sir?', 'Go to hell!', 'Of course, sir' – and off he goes. His ignorance of how to land the machine at all takes him across the Alps and finally, when his petrol gives out, to an oasis in the desert, by which time he has set up a world record, though we are not told in what. The sheer dottiness of most military commands is most cruelly exposed when taken literally, and that is what Švejk does all the time. Alternatively, his realistic clarity forces him to answer the advice of a comrade to 'shit on your lieutenant' with 'Yes, well, it's not as simple as that'. A remark to stand beside the reply of a soldier, who, after painting a paradisal picture of life in the ranks, is asked why he looks so depressed then, and answers, 'Well, you see, there's this war'. (Now, who made that one up?)

It was inevitable that the theatre should get its hands on the book, and when it did, adaptations came regularly, the present one being the most recent. The most successful so far seems to have been one of the earliest, that in Berlin in 1928 (a bare five years after the book's appearance) directed by Piscator, with script contributions from, among others, Brecht, at that time a fledgling dramaturg. Their starting-point was a version by Max Brod and Hans Reimann (who owned the theatrical rights), which Piscator found to be a banal, pseudo-comic farce about a batman, which relegated all Hašek's satire to the waste-paper basket, in favour of a series of squaddy jokes. By the time Piscator and his colleagues had finished with the book, they had evolved a wholly different method of dealing with its intractability. The passivity of the central character, and the continuous movement of everybody else were dealt with by a couple of 'travelators', moving strips which either carried Švejk in one direction or carried the other characters, along with the scenery – sketched built pieces or screens, even occasionally animated films, designed by Georg Grosz – in the other. This is reminiscent of Brecht's own staging of his *Caucasian Chalk Circle* some decades later, but it is remarkable that Piscator, the director, influenced later playwrights, as much as Brecht, the playwright, influenced the staging of them. The technical staging of the play won golden opinions, and the whole production, particularly Max Pallenberg's central performance as Švejk, was seen as a breakthrough in the modern theatre.

One question never really resolved in the production, and it is a question that hangs over the book as well, was, how much did Švejk realise his own idiocy? Did he really not know what he was saying and doing, was he taking the war and all authority *ad absurdum* by his simplicity, or was he acting with absolute consciousness? It is always difficult to believe that stupidity, or, in this case, naivety, can be quite as pronounced as it sometimes is – we always think the person in question is having us on, and it is precisely this ambiguity that makes Švejk finally into the multi-layered character he is. The mere existence of such a creature is enough to demolish every concept of authority – Church, State, Army, all of them. It is necessary for Sancho Panza to retain a native mother-wit to counterbalance in some measure the fog that fills Quixote's mind, if only to preserve his master and retain his job, but Švejk is under no such pressure; self-preservation is the only necessity. Švejk is no revolutionary fighting for a new world order – he is an entirely asocial figure, who would be just as dangerous, or, equally, just as assimilable, in a Communist world as in the decaying monarchy of Franz Joseph. His obstinate, tireless approval and acceptance of the way things are, reduce them to ineffective formulae. If Mephistopheles was, on his own admission, 'the spirit that denies', then Švejk is the spirit that agrees, and shows thereby, in equally Mephistophelian fashion, that everything that exists is worth the destruction.

Some fifteen years later, Brecht took the idea a stage further in his *Schweik in the Second World War*, a perfectly logical step, if in rather poster-colour terms. When he was in the USA, he was interested in reviving the older version, until rather sharply reminded by Piscator of his, and other collaborators' prior claim.

Kurt Weill had also been interested for some time, since the completion of his opera *Mahagonny*, in writing a comic opera on Švejk, again to a text by Brecht. When Weill got in touch with the lawyers to secure the rights, he found they were controlled by not one but two widows, Hašek having clearly been more than a little cloudy about marital arrangements – Sir Cecil Parrott, one of his translators, stated categorically that Hašek was a bigamist. The opera project's long and complicated ancestry is dealt with in David Drew's biography of Weill. What is clear is that success did not make either collaborator easier to deal with – "I have known Brecht for years. He has always been the most difficult man to work with. I had hoped he might have changed his attitude. Unfortunately I was mistaken." – Weill on 19 January 1944, by which time the project had changed in favour of a musical on *The Good Woman of Setzuan*, another project doomed to founder.

It is sad to have been done out of a Weill opera on Švejk, but Brecht, never one to let grass grow under his feet, salvaged material ('I am a great scissors-and-paste man', he used to say) from this and other Švejk-connected projects. In 1942-3 he wrote his *Schweik in the Second World War*, first produced in the winter of 1956 by the Polish Army Theatre in Warsaw. In this version, scenes show Švejk making his way through, for instance, Gestapo HQ, military prison and, finally, the Russian front, without ever betraying whether his stupidity is real or a sham. These are interlarded with short 'Interludes in The Higher Regions', where Hitler and the Nazi top-brass discuss Hitler's concern with the feelings of the Common Man towards him in Austria, Czechoslovakia, 'or whatever those countries used to be called, it doesn't matter'. While the separate scenes are roughly in the spirit of the novel, it cannot be said that the piece works well as a whole, despite the presence of several first-class songs including *The Soldier's Wife*, set by Weill, originally for a charity concert, and others by Hanns Eisler.

There were, of course, other versions of Švejk – significantly, not in Britain, though Joan Littlewood did produce *Schweik* for the Theatre Workshop – and Colin Teevan's will surely not be the last. It has not made the mistake of denying its origins as a novel: the use of literary tricks, cutting continually into the so-called dramatic texture, ensures that we, the audience, are always aware of that. Like every good adaptor, he has gone, pick in hand, to the book and hacked out what is useful to his purpose, and left the rest. Every book worth treating in this way is like a quarry, from which later ages will mine what they wish, and if this results in distortion, that will just be the way things are. The theatre can be a distorting medium, but more importantly, it only truly exists for the time it takes to perform, the speed at which it dates, and becomes unacceptable, surely being proof enough of this.

Meanwhile, Švejk, with his inexhaustible repertoire of exemplary stories, which occur to him at every turn – like Sancho Panza's proverbs, Rabelaisian anecdotes of human frailty and stupidity, a plumber's idea of the Thousand and One Nights – marches on to Budějovice, or wherever, carrying on his back his deadly obedience. In much the same way his creator bore his genius on his back, like a hump. Like it or not, religion and patriotism are the last means, if all else fails, of deceiving unsuspecting, simple people. Many of them are indeed happy to be so deceived, but it takes something like heroism to point it out.

Robert David MacDonald
Glasgow, 1999

ŠVEJK

Characters

LOUDHAILER
GRAMOPHONE
TIME
MRS PALIVEC
ŠVEJK
MR PALIVEC
MR BRETSCHNEIDER
A STATIONER
A GAMBLER
A DISINTERESTED MAN
SERGEANT ONE
SERGEANT TWO
JUDGE
A MEDICAL ORDERLY
VIRGIN MARY
EMPEROR FRANZ JOSEF
VARIOUS EUROPEAN NOTABLES
AN ARMY DOCTOR
A MOB
THE PRAGUE NEWS
LIEUTENANT DUB
A CORPORAL
LIEUTENANT LUKÁŠ
VARIOUS MALINGERERS
A DOCTOR
CHAPLAIN KATZ
A DROSHKY DRIVER
FOOTNOTE
AN ANGORA CAT
A HARZ CANARY
MISTRESS KATY

THE LETTER
THE REPLY
VODIČKA
A MAID
EMPRESS
GENERAL KRAUS
THE TRAIN
VARIOUS OLD WOMEN
VARIOUS HAYSTACKS
COLONEL SCHRÖDER
LIEUTENANT KRETSCHMANN
VARIOUS SOLDIERS
A PROSTITUTE
MR KÁKONYI
A DRUNKEN HUNGARIAN SOLDIER
AN INTELLIGENCE OFFICER
CAPTAIN SÁGNER
THE COOK
MAREK
A PUMP
LIEUTENANT DUB'S INNARDS
ST PETER
FLEEING GALICIAN PEASANTS

All parts, apart from those of ŠVEJK and LIEUTENANT LUKÁŠ, may be played variously by a chorus comprising seven or more actors.

Švejk was first performed at the Gate Theatre, London, on the 7th May 1999 with the following cast:

ŠVEJK, Martin Savage

LUKÁŠ, Ben Price

Other parts played by the following actors:

Mike Burnside, Peter Vickers, Martin Wimbush, Michael Glenn Murphy, Roy Smiles, Michael Jarvis, Gary Dunnington, Sam Bond, Maitland Chandler, Sally Hawkins, Jeanne Hepple, Benjamin Hall

Director, Dalia Ibelhauptaite

Designer, Giles Cadle

Music, David Benke

Lighting Design, Simon Mills

Assistant Director, Stephen Wisker

Note:

This playscript went to press before opening night and therefore may differ slightly from the text as performed.

Acknowledgements:

The author wishes to thank Dalia Ibelhauptaite, Mick Gordon and the Gate Theatre for their help and encouragement in the writing of this piece, and Dr Olga Smirnova for her help and advice on the Czech original.

ACT ONE

LOUDHAILER: Wind her up!

GRAMOPHONE: Great epochs call for great men;
  A hero, but not the type who, when
  He hears the calling of his nation,
  Seeks only to improve his situation,
  Like Alexander, Caesar, or Bonaparte;
  No, our hero is the little man who sees not his part
  In the cavalcade of history –

Scratch. Jump.

  – In Prague by selling dogs and drinking beer.
  And if you should chance upon him here,
  He'll tell you plain and simple; "I am Švejk"
  And tell you what he'd like
  To drink –

Jump.

  – from me, no more.
  Ladies and Gentlemen,
  The Good Soldier Švejk and his Fortunes in the War.

Crackle. Hiss.

LOUDHAILER: Six o'clock before the war!

TIME: Ding. Ding. Ding. Ding. Ding. Ding. (*Pause.*) Tick-tock.

MRS PALIVEC: So they've killed Ferdinand.

ŠVEJK: Would that be Ferdinand the chemist, Mrs Palivec, or Ferdinand the dog shit collector?

MRS PALIVEC: The Archduke, Franzie Ferdinand. Your Velkopopovický, Mr Švejk.

MR PALIVEC: A cunt on your big gob woman. The likes of us should mind our own business.

21

TIME: Tick-tock.

MRS PALIVEC: Only saying.

TIME: Tick –

ŠVEJK: That's it then, isn't it?

TIME: Tock.

BRETSCHNEIDER: What is what, Mr Švejk?

MR PALIVEC: Evening Mr Bretschneider, the usual?

BRETSCHNEIDER: What is what, Mr Švejk?

ŠVEJK: The start of it, Mr Bretschneider.

MR PALIVEC: One Velkopopovický for Mr Bretschneider, woman.

ŠVEJK: It was probably the Turks. Because of Bosnia-Herzegovina. And the Germans are bound to stick up for the Turks. But the Russians hate the Turks and they'll go with us. And as for the French, with 1871 and all that, they'll be with us too. Though then the Kaiser and the King of England are cousins and blood is thicker –

MR PALIVEC: Like they say Mr Švejk, little pigs... drink your beer if you please.

ŠVEJK: Right you are, Mr Palivec.

TIME: Tick-tock.

BRETSCHNEIDER: You seem very sure, Mr Švejk.

ŠVEJK: Stands to reason. I once knew of a gamekeeper in Zliv. Some poachers shot him. Left a wife and two kids. What else could she do but marry another game-keeper? But didn't that gamekeeper go and get himself shot too. And so she married a third and same again. Poor woman had six children by now and sensed

22

that she was not destined to find marital bliss with a gamekeeper so she plumped for a pond attendant from Ražice, but didn't he go and fall in the drink and drown. So finally she took up with a pig gelder from Vodňany who, one night, knocked her dead with his castrating equipment. And at his trial the pig gelder bit the judge's nose and said some very nasty things about Emperor Franz Josef. They hung him out to dry. So if his Majesty won't stand for that from a castrator of pigs from Vodňany, he's not going to let a Turk go round bumping off his nearest and dearest.

MR PALIVEC: For once and –

BRETSCHNEIDER: What sort of things, Mr Švejk?

ŠVEJK: What sort of what things, Mr Bretschneider?

BRETSCHNEIDER: What sort of unflattering things did this pig gelder say, Mr Švejk?

MR PALIVEC: Who's for another Velkopopovický?

ŠVEJK: Don't mind if I –

BRETSCHNEIDER: Forget the bloody Velkopopovický. What did this pig gelder say?

ŠVEJK: I can't say exactly, Mr Bretschneider, sir.

BRETSCHNEIDER: Well say roundaboutly, Mr Švejk.

ŠVEJK: I cannot, Mr Bretschneider, recall even the roundabouts of it.

BRETSCHNEIDER: Tell me the jist then, Mr Švejk.

ŠVEJK: I'm sorry, Mr Bretschneider sir, even the jist eludes me.

MR PALIVEC: Drink your beers –

BRETSCHNEIDER: Palivec, didn't you once have a picture of the Emperor on the wall?

MR PALIVEC: I did, Mr Bretschneider, but I had to take it down. (*Pause.*) The flies used shit on it something rotten.

TIME: Tick-tock-tick.

BRETSCHNEIDER: Little pigs with big ears, eh?

Pause.

TIME: Bring-aling-a-ling-a-ling!

LOUDHAILER: A STATE OF EMERGENCY!

A state of emergency is enacted.

TIME: Bring-aling-a-ling-a-ling!

Pause.

A STATIONER: Let me go, I'm innocent. I've got children.

A GAMBLER: – Minding my own business, I was. Game of whist. Down to the last card. King of Spades he played. But he'd miscounted. Three of trumps, says I. Bang, bang, bang, I says, like Ferdinand in Sarajevo. I win!

A DISINTERESTED MAN: – "So have you seen the news?" he says sitting down uninvited like. "Nope," I say. "So you don't know?" he says. "Nope," I say. "You're not even interested?" he says. "Nope," I say. "Well, you should be," he says. "I'm not interested in nothing," I say. "I'm a disinterested man." "Not even the murder in Sarajevo?" "Nope," I say. "If someone wants to get themselves shot in Sarajevo, that's their own look-out. Bloody fools."

MR PALIVEC: A cunt on those flies. I mind my own business. That's what I do. I sell beer and mind my own business. The poxy bastards.

A STATIONER: Let me go, let me go, I'm innocent.

ŠVEJK: So was Jesus Christ.

A GAMBLER: And look what they did to him.

A DISINTERESTED MAN: As if it mattered.

A STATIONER: O God, let me go. I'm a stationer.

A DISINTERESTED MAN: That's no excuse. I'm completely disinterested and look at me.

ŠVEJK: What are the police there for if not to punish us when we speak out of turn? I mean if Archdukes are going around getting shot, these are dangerous times. We can't be trusted to trust ourselves. Someone must maintain law and order.

A STATIONER: But I'm innocent, I demand justice.

ŠVEJK: A woman in Putim was once sentenced for strangling her newborn twins although both she and the midwife swore she'd only given birth to one little girl who, she freely admitted, she'd suffocated without any trouble. She was still hung for double murder.

A door opens, a SERGEANT'S FINGER points.

THE SERGEANT'S FINGER: Švejk!

ŠVEJK: Me? But some of these other men have been waiting much longer. Take our stationer friend, for example –

A STATIONER: What stationer? What would a stationer be doing in a place like this? Stationary is a respectable profession.

ŠVEJK is hauled before the two investigating SERGEANTS.

SERGEANT TWO: Take that idiotic expression off your face.

ŠVEJK: I can't. I was discharged from National Service for stupidity and officially certified by a special commission as an idiot. I am an official idiot.

SERGEANT TWO: Did you hear that?

SERGEANT ONE: I heard that.

SERGEANT TWO: He's trying to be clever with us.

SERGEANT ONE: You shouldn't try and be clever with us.

ŠVEJK: I couldn't be clever with you, even if I wanted –

SERGEANT ONE: Now he's taking the piss.

SERGEANT TWO: He thinks he's clever.

SERGEANT ONE: We should teach him not to take the piss.

SERGEANT TWO: We should teach him not to be clever.

SERGEANT ONE: Smell this, you scum!

SERGEANT ONE punches him on the nose.

ŠVEJK: Thank you, sir.

SERGEANT TWO: So, what did you smell on the Sergeant's fist, scum?

ŠVEJK: The boneyard.

SERGEANT TWO: Good. Now, do you admit to your crimes detailed by Secret Detective Bretschneider?

ŠVEJK: I admit to everything. You've got to be strict. Without strictness where would we be? When I was doing my national service –

SERGEANT TWO: Shut your ugly mug, scum. Make him shut his ugly mug, Sergeant.

SERGEANT ONE: Right you are, Sergeant.

SERGEANT ONE punches him on the nose again.

SERGEANT TWO: Now, are you willing to sign this confession?

ŠVEJK: If you say so.

SERGEANT TWO: I do.

SERGEANT ONE: We do.

ŠVEJK: Right you are. Yours faithfully Josef Švejk.

SERGEANT ONE: You know, Sergeant, it's almost no fun anymore.

ŠVEJK: I'm sorry.

SERGEANT TWO: You shut it! You've upset the Sergeant enough.

SERGEANT ONE: Thank you, Sergeant. You'll be taken to the district court for sentencing at six tomorrow morning. Anything to say, scum?

ŠVEJK: Six o'clock in the morning is very early. Can I have an alarm clock?

SERGEANT TWO: He's doing it again, Sergeant.

SERGEANT ONE: He mustn't be able to smell too well.

SERGEANT TWO: Let's teach him, let's clear his nasal passage, Sergeant.

SERGEANT ONE & SERGEANT TWO: Smell this and this and this!

ŠVEJK: Long live Emperor Franz Josef.

ŠVEJK is beaten.

Long live...

They have retreated. Pause.

(*Sings.*) AT THE DARKEST HOUR OF NIGHT,
WHEN ALL THE WORLD IS SLEEPING TIGHT,
MY LOVE WHISPERS IN MY EAR,

"TIS TIME TO PUT OFF ALL YOUR FEAR."
                HOLD ME,
                HOLD ME –

A heavenly light, a CHOIR sings. The JUDGE enters.

JUDGE: Do you feel alright, Mr Švejk?

ŠVEJK: Now that you mention it, your honour, my rheumatism's at me again.

JUDGE: Well, Mr Švejk, for a man with rheumatism, you've certainly been busy.

ŠVEJK: I do my best to keep body and soul together. I sell dogs. Poms, Pinschers you name it.

JUDGE: Is that so?

ŠVEJK: There's nothing you couldn't tell me about them. I pick up mongrels and strays and all sorts of goulash bastards and paint their hair with silver nitrate. And, if the animal's old, I feed it arsenic so that it will get some strength back and I clean its teeth with sand-paper and just before I hand it over to the new owner I give it a shot of slivovitz so that it jumps around like a puppy...

Pause.

JUDGE: And in between business commitments you managed to assassinate his Royal Highness Franz Ferdinand?

ŠVEJK: If that's what it says, I will not deny it.

JUDGE: Did they bring any pressure to bear on you at police headquarters?

ŠVEJK: Of course not, sir. At least none that I did not deserve. They asked me to sign, and I said of course. We must co-operate with our police force or what kind of state would we be in?

JUDGE: Perhaps you need a little rest.

A MEDICAL ORDERLY begins to undress ŠVEJK.

ŠVEJK: Now that you mention it, I do feel a bit tired. I'm having to use my room as a kennel at present and a German shepherd, who used to be a collie mongrel, had me awake half the night trying it on with a poodle, who is some kind of terrier pom crossbreed I've been preparing for a blind woman from Vráž, your honour. Your honour?

MEDICAL ORDERLY: (*Escorting ŠVEJK away.*) The undersigned medical experts certify the complete mental decrepitude of Josef Švejk –

LOUDHAILER: And the angel of the Lord declared unto Mary –

ALL: And she grew fat by the Holy Spirit.

The VIRGIN MARY goes into labour. She is attended by the CROWNED HEADS of Europe and other NOTABLES. It is a difficult birth. The VIRGIN MARY curses her luck while the dignitaries sing "Ave Maria".

VIRGIN MARY: Jesus! Jesus!

ŠVEJK emerges from between the VIRGIN MARY's legs.

LOUDHAILER: In the mad house, the new age was born.

VIRGIN MARY: (*At the sight of ŠVEJK.*) Christ!

LOUDHAILER: It was a terrible beauty.

They bathe ŠVEJK.

ŠVEJK: In my later years I will always recall with fondness my days in the lunatic asylum. There's liberty not even Socialists have dreamed of. You can be the King of England, the Pope, The Tsar, even our own Emperor. One man is both St. Cyril and St. Methodius and thereby gets double portions at tea. And as for your behaviour; you can kick, you can crawl, you can fight, you can yell, you can dance or even just bark like a mad dog for all you're worth and no-one will tell you to shut up or that you should be ashamed of yourself or that this is no proper way to behave. And they wash you and scrub you and trim your nails so that you're as rosy and pink as the day you were born –

EMPEROR FRANZ JOSEF: So, little man, who are you?

ŠVEJK: I am Švejk, your Imperial Majesty Franz Josef.

EMPEROR FRANZ JOSEF: Švejk? Švejk? What is a Švejk?

ŠVEJK: Me, your Majesty.

EMPEROR FRANZ JOSEF: But is it anything?

ŠVEJK: I'm not sure, your Majesty, I've never really amounted to very much.

EMPEROR FRANZ JOSEF: Well, little man, you should know that in here you must be someone. Anyone who's anyone is here. And if you're not anyone, you're no one and you've no place being somewhere like this.

ŠVEJK: But I like it here, your Majesty.

EMPEROR FRANZ JOSEF: Well then you must do better than this Švejk character.

ŠVEJK: I'll try... No, I'm sorry. I can't come up with anything better. I fear I'll always be a Švejk.

EMPEROR FRANZ JOSEF: You won't last long.

DOCTOR: Name?

ŠVEJK: Švejk.

DOCTOR: What?

ŠVEJK: Švejk.

DOCTOR: Come on, you don't expect me to fall for that. How can you possibly believe that you are this Švejk character?

ŠVEJK: My mother was Mrs Švejk and my father was Mr Švejk. I would not wish to insult their memory by denying their part in my existence.

DOCTOR: Well then Mr Švejk, could you please tell me whether radium is heavier than lead?

ŠVEJK: Yes, because I can lift a lead pencil quite easily, but I've never managed to lift a radium one –

DOCTOR: Do you believe in the end of the world?

ŠVEJK: I believe the world is round, so it can have no end.

DOCTOR: I'm sorry to say, you've failed.

ŠVEJK: I know I have. I've never been much good at anything.

DOCTOR: You have no delusions and your answers are stupid enough as to have a grain of sense to them. I must discharge you.

ŠVEJK: Why? I like it here. How can you discharge me?

DOCTOR: I am a doctor. You're completely sane.

ŠVEJK: But I'm an idiot.

DOCTOR: Prove it.

ŠVEJK: Prove you're a doctor?

DOCTOR: You see, far too sensible a reply. Please have this man removed.

A MEDICAL ORDERLY enters and removes ŠVEJK.

ŠVEJK: But I was having such a nice time –

DOCTOR: This isn't a holiday resort; this is madness. Now, all of you, get back to what you were doing.

The inmates sing 'For unto us a child is born' from Handel's <u>Messiah</u>.

LOUDHAILER: And a door closed on the episode.

A door closes on the episode.

ŠVEJK: (*Kicking against the closed door.*) But you can't discharge me. I haven't had my dinner. I haven't had my dinner. I want my dinner! Let me back in!

SERGEANT ONE and SERGEANT TWO come across the outraged ŠVEJK.

SERGEANT TWO: You again, you scum!

SERGEANT ONE: He's causing a disturbance again, Sergeant.

SERGEANT TWO: Kicking up a rumpus at the puzzle factory? Teach him not to kick up a rumpus at the puzzle factory, Sergeant.

SERGEANT ONE: Haven't you had a good enough smell of my fist yet, scum?

SERGEANT TWO: It's the pit for you, matey.

ŠVEJK is thrown into the pit. Marching feet are heard offstage. Long pause. From the gloom MR PALIVEC gradually becomes visible.

ŠVEJK: Mr Palivec? Is that you? It's me, Švejk. I'm back again.

MR PALIVEC: You? You cunt!

ŠVEJK: Yes, it's me. How have you been?

MR PALIVEC: How do you think, you stupid bastard? Ten years they've given me. All I did was tell the judge that I didn't give an Emperor's flying toss for politics. All I ever wanted to do was sell beer.

ŠVEJK: Don't worry, it will all blow over in a couple of weeks. They've got to keep things in order till then. And while we're waiting for it to blow over, we can just carry on like it's not happening. You don't want to get excessively upset or worked up about what you can't control. (*Pause.*) It reminds me of a trick the Pope taught us to play in the asylum. At exercise time in the yard we'd all decide on a number. "Thirteen", for example. And then we'd shout it at the top of our voices.

ALL: (*Off.*) "Thirteen! Thirteen! Thirteen!"

ŠVEJK: And passers-by would get curious and say to themselves, "I wonder what's going on in there that everyone's shouting thirteen." And there was this hole in the wall. And passers-by couldn't resist having a look. And, quick as a flash the Pope would poke the curious passer-by in the eye with his staff of St. Peter. It was really some piping from the jacks. And then we'd all shout –

ALL: (*Off.*) "Fourteen! Fourteen!"

ŠVEJK: It's just like that. It's best not to look. (*Pause.*) You know, this is like old times, isn't it? At your pub. Before it all began. Six o'clock.

MR PALIVEC: If you ever get back there, tell my wife she's a stupid cow and that if this stinking mess has an upside, it's that I won't have to put up with her anymore.

ŠVEJK: Yes, Mr Palivec, I'll try and remember…

MR PALIVEC: Give us your belt you poxy whorescunt.

ŠVEJK: Yes, Mr Palivec, of course. (*He does so. Trousers around ankles.*) Only don't be too long, it's quite damp in this pit and my rheumatism has been playing up. Mr Palivec?

MR PALIVEC is hanged.

Mr Palivec?

Pause.

JUDGE: Do you feel alright, Mr Švejk?

ŠVEJK: Yes your honour.

JUDGE: What brings you here again?

ŠVEJK: I appear to be trapped in a vicious circle.

JUDGE: We must have you taken home. I will arrange for you to be accompanied so that you can break this circle of crime once and for all.

ŠVEJK: Yes sir, thank you sir.

Marching offstage is heard once more.

What's that noise, your honour?

LOUDHAILER: And the truth marched out across Europe; tomorrow would obliterate the plans of today.

ŠVEJK: Just as I predicted.

LOUDHAILER: All over Europe, the lights –

The lights go out.

(*In darkness.*) – went out.

Pause.

MRS PALIVEC: (*Sobbing in darkness.*) He was a sweet man, really. Simple desires.

Lights on.

ŠVEJK: I'm back, Mrs Palivec. It's me, Švejk.

MRS PALIVEC: All he wanted to do was sell beer.

ŠVEJK: Don't worry, Mrs Palivec. It will be over by Christmas. A Velkopopovický, please.

MRS PALIVEC: (*Mournfully.*) One Velkopopovický.

She opens a bottle.

By the way, this arrived for you last week while you were away.

ŠVEJK: (*Reading, announces.*) I'm going to war.

MRS PALIVEC: You? But you can't move for the rheumatism in your legs.

ŠVEJK: Well, apart from that I'm completely sound cannon fodder. I'll go to war in a bath chair if necessary. Yes, a bath chair. My fatherland needs me. Fetch me a bath chair, Mrs Palivec, and one Velkopopovický for the road. To Belgrade!

(*Sings.*) GENERAL WINDISCHGRÄTZ, AT THE DAWN OF DAY,
DREW HIS SWORD AND JOINED THE FRAY
WITH A HOP, HOP, HOP!

WITH SWORD ALOFT AND GOD ON HIS SIDE,
HE SPURRED HIS MEN TO FIGHT WITH PRIDE
WITH A HOP, HOP, HOP!

"WITH GOD ON YOUR SIDE AND CASH IN THE CART
YOU'LL BE DANCING TONIGHT WITH A VILLAGE TART
WITH A HOP, HOP, HOP!

DANCE AS THE DEAD GROW STIFF IN THE PARK,

IT'S A FUNNY OLD LIFE THIS SOLDIERING LARK.
NOW HOP, HOP, HOP!"

*ŠVEJK sings along in a bath chair and is joined by a
MOB. They sing too.*

To Belgrade!

MOB: Hurrah!

ŠVEJK: To Belgrade!

MOB: Hurrah!

ŠVEJK: To Belgrade!

THE PRAGUE NEWS: A Cripple's Patriotism. Yesterday
evening the passers-by in the streets of Prague were
witnesses to an extraordinary scene of loyalty to the
cause of his Majesty Franz Josef –

ŠVEJK: Long live Franz Josef, long live Franz Josef, long
live –

ŠVEJK has arrived at the draft board.

DUB: Enough of that! I can see right through you, you
malingering toe-rag. I am Lieutenant Dub. You don't
know me yet, but stand out of line and you'll get to know
me alright. Now, Corporal, what's his story –

CORPORAL: Permission to report, certified as unfit for
service on the grounds of idiocy, Lieutenant Dub, sir.

DUB: A likely bloody story.

ŠVEJK: And, 'mission to report, I've got rheumatism, sir.

DUB: Rheumatism! Idiocy! You know, it will be a bloody
miracle if we don't get the better of you. The army gets
the better of everyone. The army is the iron fist in the
velvet glove of his Majesty's rule which is a jackboot

which will crush all opposition like a hammer. Do I make myself clear, Švejk?

ŠVEJK: Yes sir, I want to die for his Majesty Franz Josef.

DUB: A likely bloody story. I'd like to know what it is you think you are thinking?

ŠVEJK: 'Mission to report, sir, I don't think.

DUB: What do you mean you don't think?

ŠVEJK: 'Mission to report, when I was doing my national service our captain always used to say, "a soldier mustn't think for himself. His superiors must think for him. As soon as a soldier starts to think he is no longer a soldier but a stinking civilian, sir" –

DUB: Shut your face, shut your ugly face, do you hear me? I know you, I know your game. You're no idiot, you're a sly little fox, you malingering bastard. To the underpants with him.

CORPORAL: But sir, he's an official idiot.

DUB: What?

CORPORAL: Permission to report, we shouldn't have idiots in the army, Lieutenant Dub, sir, surely.

Pause. DUB shoots CORPORAL.

DUB: That will teach you to talk out of turn, Corporal. And let that be a lesson to you too.

LUKÁŠ runs in.

LUKÁŠ: Everything alright, Lieutenant Dub? I heard gunfire.

DUB: Just administering some basic training, Lieutenant Lukáš.

LUKÁŠ: I see. But the corporal – ?

DUB: Cramps. Any complaints, corporal? (*Pause.*) See, no complaints.

Pause. LUKÁŠ notices ŠVEJK. ŠVEJK notices LUKÁŠ.

LUKÁŠ: And you, soldier?

ŠVEJK: 'Mission to report, sir, I am completely satisfied.

LUKÁŠ: Yes, very well then. I'll be... off.

MALINGERERS on potties, underpants around their ankles.

MALINGERERS: (*Singing.*) O AUSTRIA MY FATHERLAND,
YOUR BANNERS RAISE UP HIGH.
YOUR TERRITORIES WE WILL DEFEND,
FOR YOU WE'LL GLADLY DIE.

ARMY DOCTOR: So, you bastards, what does life look like with a double enema up your arse.

MALINGERERS: We are completely satisfied, Doctor, sir.

ARMY DOCTOR: Glad to hear it. Back to work then.

They heave. One man heaves his last.

A MALINGERER: Third this week.

ANOTHER MALINGERER: He didn't last long.

ŠVEJK: We all must do our bit for the war effort. We should count ourselves lucky. When I did my service they used to truss us together and hang us in a hole. I was once tied to a man who had smallpox.

They heave.

ANOTHER MALINGERER: So, what's your excuse?

ŠVEJK: Rheumatism.

A MALINGERER: Ha!

ANOTHER MALINGERER: You won't last long.

YET ANOTHER MALINGERER: Rheumatism. He won't last long.

A MALINGERER: I've lost half my stomach and five ribs and no one believes me.

ANOTHER MALINGERER: I've got cancer of the brain.

YET ANOTHER MALINGERER: I had a midwife in Vršovice dislocate my legs for twenty crowns.

ŠVEJK: What about him?

A MALINGERER: Epilepsy.

ANOTHER MALINGERER: He won't last long either.

YET ANOTHER MALINGERER: It's the foaming. Don't pick an illness that involves foaming.

A MALINGERER: They had a stroke victim up and off to the front after only two enemas.

ANOTHER MALINGERER: He didn't last long.

They heave.

A MALINGERER: At least it's Sunday.

ŠVEJK: What happens on Sunday?

KATZ: (*Entering on a pulpit, drunk.*) Right you lousy stinking shower of cowardly putrescence; Dominus vobiscum. Now, pull up your pants, you shitbuckets, you are in the temple of the lord not a pissoir. Right, let's start with a bloody song.

(*Sings.*) I LOVE HER LIKE THE LIGHT OF DAY;
A LOVE SO PURE AND UNCONTRARY.
SHE WATCHES ME, SHE LIGHTS MY WAY,
SHE'S THE BLESSED VIRGIN MARY.
YES SHE'S MY OWN BLESSED VIRGIN MARY.

You bastards are human beings, I suppose, and see the truth, if at all, if there is in fact any truth to be seen, you see it through a dark glass. The spirit glass – you know I should pray for your damned souls, that our saviour might wash away your sins with his eternal love, and all that. But that's where you're wrong, because I couldn't be arsed with such a crew of bastardy cunts as you lot. Any complaints with that?

MALINGERERS: 'Mission to report, Chaplain Katz, we have no complaints. We are completely satisfied.

KATZ: Even God's goodness has its limits. He is merciful, but only to decent people, not cowardly, heathen scum like yourselves. You don't know your prayers, you think going to church is about having a bit of a laugh –

KATZ falls.

KATZ: What am I doing wasting my time with you? You are all damned. Damned, damned –

The underpants heave. One is weeping.

KATZ: What's that? Who's snivelling?

ŠVEJK: 'Mission to report, it's me, sir.

KATZ: Right, well, stop it. I can't stand seeing a grown man snivel.

ŠVEJK: Yes, Chaplain Katz, sir.

KATZ: And the rest of you, take example from this bastard. At least one of you wants to become a better man. I've had enough. Dominus vobiscum. Now abtreten and bugger off. Except you.

ŠVEJK: ?

KATZ: Yes, you little shit. What do you mean by taking the piss?

ŠVEJK: 'Mission to report, I was not taking the piss, sir.

KATZ: Jesus, you weren't being genuine, were you?

ŠVEJK: 'Mission to report, I was not being genuine either.

KATZ: Then you were taking the piss.

ŠVEJK: 'Mission to report sir, I was putting it on alright, but only because I felt that your sermon needed a reformed sinner and when no-one volunteered I took it upon myself – you seemed to be despairing a little of humanity's ability to reform itself –

KATZ: I'm beginning to warm to you.

ŠVEJK: Thank you, sir.

KATZ: Can you make a good grog?

ŠVEJK: The best. I used to know a journalist, Hašek, he wrote for The Animal News. He gave me his recipe.

FOOTNOTE: (*Appears and salutes.*) Footnote, sir. Hašek's personal recipe for the making of a good grog. "Boil up half a litre of water, three allspice corns, eight peppercorns, ten cloves, a cinnamon stick, grated lemon rind. Add a pound of sugar. After boiling, add six pints of white wine and two pints of cognac and bring it near boiling point again. Remove pot to table, light the vapours, quench flames then drink. And if someone tells you to add vanilla, give him one in the face."

KATZ: You, you footnoting bastard, bugger off, and you... (*To ŠVEJK.*) I'll have a word with whoever's in charge of this stinking mess. Here, put on this uniform. That little performance of yours has potential. Together we will lead the lost sheep into the fields of Elysium like lambs of God to the slaughter.

ŠVEJK: Yes sir, Chaplain Katz, sir, I will serve you till my dying breath.

A DROSHKY DRIVER and his droshky.

KATZ: I demand you take me to Rome, you cunt!

DROSHKY DRIVER: Piss off, Padre. You spewed all over my droshky Tuesday was a week.

KATZ: Listen you pignoramus, I'll see to it that you'll lose your license. I am not without influence you know...

ŠVEJK: (*Arriving.*) Sorry about this. Here's a crown. Just take us home.

DROSHKY DRIVER: Right, but watch that pisswit doesn't spew, that's all I'm saying.

ŠVEJK and KATZ get in.

ŠVEJK: 'Mission to report, Chaplain Katz, this is the sixth time this week.

KATZ: Who are you anyhow?

ŠVEJK: I am your batman, your reverence. I've come to take you home.

KATZ: I haven't got a batman, and I have no reverence. I'm a dog. Miaow. Let me go, I don't know you. I've been with the archbishop. The Vatican's interested in me. Leave me alone. Help! Kidnap!

DROSHKY DRIVER: Is he spewing?

ŠVEJK: He's my brother. I've been at the front. He thought I was dead and he was so happy to see me, he got drunk.

DROSHKY DRIVER: I don't give a five knuckle shuffle who he is, just watch him, right.

KATZ: Whosoever of you is dead must report to Army Corps headquarters within three days so that your corpse can be sprinkled with holy water.

ŠVEJK punches KATZ in the ribs.

ŠVEJK: Will you keep it down or we'll never get home.

KATZ: Yes. Yes. Thank you. I needed that. In Budějovice there once was a drummer. He got married. A year later he died. Isn't that a good story? Eh? I'm all alone in this world. Mummy! I am a dog. Moo! Give me one in the eye.

ŠVEJK: Is that an order?

KATZ: Yes.

ŠVEJK gives KATZ one in the eye.

KATZ: Thank you. I feel a bit better.

ŠVEJK: We're home.

KATZ: My guardian angel. I love you. You are my saviour. Don't ever leave me.

ŠVEJK: No, sir.

A game of cards. As it progresses KATZ loses his watch, his cufflinks, his crucifix and his shirt to LUKÁŠ. He is cleaned out. The game continues. LUKÁŠ goes to take the pot. KATZ stops him. KATZ gestures ŠVEJK onto the table. ŠVEJK obliges. The cards are seen, KATZ has lost.

KATZ: Švejk, what have I done? I have lost you. Curse me. Beat me, I'll take it. I'll enjoy it. Please, please don't look at me like that. Like an innocent child. I can't bear it. Do what you want to me, give me one in the eye, both eyes, but take that look off your face.

ŠVEJK: 'Mission to report, but how much am I worth, sir?

KATZ: 100 crowns give or take a few kreutzers.

ŠVEJK: I received my back-pay, today, sir. A hundred crowns. I can lend you 100 crowns to buy me back.

KATZ: A hundred crowns? Why didn't you say, my boy? You truly are an angel of mercy. Give it here. I'll win everything back, you'll see.

ŠVEJK: But, 'mission to report, Chaplain Katz, sir –

KATZ: Deal, Lieutenant. I feel lucky tonight.

KATZ loses all the money then resigns himself to his fate and signals ŠVEJK onto the table. He has lost everything. He looks at ŠVEJK for a moment, then takes his leave wearing nothing but his dog collar. A silence. LUKÁŠ stands. ŠVEJK stands up on table and salutes. Pause. ŠVEJK climbs down from table and salutes. LUKÁŠ goes to sit down. ŠVEJK pulls chair out for him. LUKÁŠ sits on ŠVEJK's hand. LUKÁŠ notices he is sitting on ŠVEJK's hand, he stands up. ŠVEJK pulls chair back for LUKÁŠ, LUKÁŠ sits, falls on floor, grabs chair from ŠVEJK, sits down. Pause. ŠVEJK salutes again.

ŠVEJK: 'Mission to report, Lieutenant...

LUKÁŠ: Lukáš. Lieutenant Lukáš.

ŠVEJK: Yes sir, Lieutenant Lukáš, sir.

LUKÁŠ: Haven't we...?

ŠVEJK: Yes sir, Lieutenant Lukáš, at the draft board. When the corporal...

LUKÁŠ: That's it.

ŠVEJK: Yes, sir.

LUKÁŠ: Indeed... well, anyway, it seems as though I have won you...

ŠVEJK: 'Mission to report, sir, Švejk, sir. Yes, you have won me, Lieutenant Lukáš, sir.

LUKÁŠ: Well, one thing you should know about me, Švejk, if you are to serve me as my batman, is that

I am firm but fair. I don't like to punish a man, but an army depends on discipline because without discipline an army is blown like a puffball hither and thither in the wind. (*Pause.*) Yes. I don't like to punish a man. I'm the type of chap who says "Look here, I don't like to punish you, old man, but I've got to, this is the army after all, and an army needs discipline or else it is blown like a puffball"... That's the kind of chap I am. You get the picture?

ŠVEJK: Yes, sir, Lieutenant Lukáš, sir, I get the picture. I will be your batman and you are firm but fair. I will serve you faithfully till my dying breath. Long live Emperor Franz Josef!

Pause.

LUKÁŠ: God, what kind of idiot has Katz palmed off on me?

ŠVEJK: 'Mission to report, a complete idiot, sir.

FOOTNOTE: (*Appears and salutes.*) Footnote, sir. The officer's batman. The officer's batman or orderly is of very ancient origin. No doubt Alexander the Great had one and what else was Don Quixote's Sancho Panza but a batman too. It is told in the memoirs of the Duke of Almavira how he was so hungry at the siege of Toledo that he ate his batman with salt. He remarked that the aforesaid batman was a tender and flavoursome soul, tasting something like a cross between a chicken and a mule. (*Pause.*) In those days of yore a batman was supposed to be virtuous, truthful and brave. The modern batman, however, is a sneaky underling who thinks of the most unusual ways to make his master's life a misery. As for these masters, they wage an infernal struggle against these batmen and, in such attritional conflicts as these, any method that serves to preserve their authority is deemed justified –

Pause. LUKÁŠ stares at FOOTNOTE. FOOTNOTE salutes and departs.

LUKÁŠ: Now listen Švejk, I've had more than a dozen batmen and not one of them has ever lasted. While I don't expect you to do any better, I am prepared to give you a chance –

ŠVEJK: 'Mission to report, sir, that is very kind, sir –

LUKÁŠ: Yes, well, the rules; first of all you should know that I come down like a ton of bricks on dishonesty –

ŠVEJK notices a HARZ CANARY and an ANGORA CAT.

ŠVEJK: 'Mission to report, Lieutenant Lukáš, sir –

LUKÁŠ: What is it now, Švejk?

ŠVEJK: Is that a Harz Canary, sir?

LUKÁŠ: What? Yes. Yes it is. I am especially fond of my pets. Animals in general.

ŠVEJK: Me too, Lieutenant Lukáš, sir. Dogs, especially.

LUKÁŠ: Is that so? Well, see to it that you treat my pets with due respect. My previous batmen used to starve them and beat them. Now, where was I?

ŠVEJK: Honesty, Lieutenant Lukáš, sir.

LUKÁŠ: Yes, thank you, I want you always to speak the truth. And carry out my orders without question. If I say jump into the fire, you jump into the fire, whether you want to jump into the fire or not.

ŠVEJK: Yes, Lieutenant Lukáš, sir. I will jump into the fire if you tell me to jump in the fire, and as for lies, the worst thing a man can do is tell a lie, because, as soon as he starts telling lies, he'll find himself in confusion because if, after telling a lie, he then tells the truth, he'll start contradicting his lie and so the only way out of the confusion is to tell more lies which leads only to more confusion.

LUKÁŠ: Yes, Švejk, exactly. So –

ŠVEJK: In a village near Pelhřimov there was a schoolmaster called Hajek who used to go with the daughter of the gamekeeper Špera. The gamekeeper warned him that if he ever caught him in the forest with the girl he'd fill his backside full of salt. The schoolmaster told him there was no truth to the rumour of a relationship, but then, once, when he was going to meet her for a secret tickle, so to speak, he met the gamekeeper. He claimed he was just picking flowers. The time after that he was caught again and he said he was just collecting dung-beetles for a science lesson. Then a third time. And this time the teacher got into a panic and said he was setting traps for hares so the gamekeeper hauled him off to the police for poaching and the case came before the courts and he was sent to prison where he died in an outbreak of typhus. Whereas, if he'd told the truth the first time, he would have just got a backside full of salt.

Pause.

LUKÁŠ: Yes, Švejk, thank you for that. Yes. And finally... Ladies sometimes pay me social visits. Sometimes they stay the night. If a lady stays the night you will bring us coffee in bed the next morning –

ŠVEJK: Yes, Lieutenant Lukáš, but, 'mission to report, perhaps we should agree on a number of knocks.

LUKÁŠ: ?

ŠVEJK: – when I come with the coffee. I once brought a lady back to my room and my landlady brought us coffee in bed, but she didn't knock and we were in the middle of having a bit of a tickle ourselves and she scalded us something rotten and that was the last I saw of the lady. (*Pause.*) Will we say three?

LUKÁŠ: I'm sorry –

ŠVEJK: Knocks. With the coffee.

LUKÁŠ: Yes, three. Whatever.

ŠVEJK: 'Mission to report, will that be all, sir?

LUKÁŠ: Yes. No. Tidy yourself up, Švejk. We might be Czechs, but the world doesn't need to know. Now, I've got some new recruits to induct. I expect the place to be spotless when I return.

ŠVEJK puts on an apron. ŠVEJK tidies room up. ŠVEJK introduces the CAT to the CANARY.

ŠVEJK: Miaow, kitty, kitty, kitty. Miaow miaow miaow. Miaow? Cheep-cheep cheep, birdy. Cheep cheep? Miaow, miaow, pussy, miaow. Cheep?

CANARY: What the hell does he think he's doing?

CAT: Ours is not to question why.

ŠVEJK: Miaow, kitty. Cheep, birdy.

CANARY: Christ, I've shitted myself.

CAT: Damn it, you'll ruin the taste.

CANARY: I'm too young to die.

CAT: The good always die young.

The CAT bites the CANARY's head off.

ŠVEJK: (*Angry with CAT.*) MIAOW! MIAOW! MIAOW! KITTY.

The CAT retreats.

LUKÁŠ: You what?

ŠVEJK: I just thought I'd try and get them to be friends. Introduce them, so to speak and he just... They say it's because they're unmusical that they don't like canaries. I gave him a sound talking to but I didn't lay a finger on him. I thought it best to wait for you to pass sentence.

CAT: Miaow?

LUKÁŠ: Are you a complete imbecile, Švejk?

ŠVEJK: I think I must be, Lieutenant Lukáš, sir. Every time I try to put something right, it goes wrong. Once, when I was a boy... Are you alright sir?

LUKÁŠ: Yes, Švejk, it's just that when you start one of your stories, I come over... I've had a long day with the new cadets. I'm on again in the morning.

ŠVEJK: Perhaps, I could mix some grog –

FOOTNOTE: (*Appears and salutes.*) Footnote, sir. Add a pound of sugar –

LUKÁŠ: Put a lid on it, for God's sake.

ŠVEJK: Yes sir.

ŠVEJK puts a lid on FOOTNOTE.

LUKÁŠ: I really think I should turn in.

CAT: Miaow.

ŠVEJK: What about the cat?

LUKÁŠ: The cat?

ŠVEJK: How do you wish to punish the cat?

LUKÁŠ: Three days solitary.

ŠVEJK: Yes, sir, Lieutenant Lukáš, sir.

LUKÁŠ: Well done, Švejk.

ŠVEJK: Thank you, sir.

CAT: (*Imprisoned, sings.*) A KDYŽ BYLO PŮL NOCI,
VOVES Z PYTLE VYSKOČÍ,
ŽUPAJDIJÁ, ŽUPAJDÁ,
KAŽDÁ HOLKA DÁ.

KATY: Knock-knock-knock. Knock-knock-knock.

A door is opened. KATY enters.

Put them in the bedroom, I'll unpack them later.

ŠVEJK: The Lieutenant is not at home.

KATY: Well, I'll wait. Now, are you going to put them in
the bedroom?

ŠVEJK: I cannot do anything without Lieutenant Lukáš'
permission.

KATY: Well then, I'll have to do it myself.

ŠVEJK: I'm afraid you can't. Lieutenant Lukáš has given
me no instructions to allow strangers to use his
apartment for the storage of luggage.

KATY: Stranger? I love Jindřich and he loves me.

ŠVEJK: Lieutenant Lukáš has not apprised me of such an
exchange of sentiment.

KATY: Where is he?

ŠVEJK: Out.

KATY: Is he at the academy?

ŠVEJK: That is confidential military information –

KATY: Listen, you fool…Right, take this letter to him and
I'll wait here.

A LETTER: Your batman is a swine and my husband
cannot give me what I want so I've decided to move in
with you. Love Katy.

ŠVEJK: I'm afraid you'll have to wait in the hall

KATY: Right, I'll wait in the hall.

ŠVEJK: With your luggage.

KATY: You double swine.

Time passes.

TIME: Tick-tock. Tick-tock. Tick-tock.

CAT: A DÁ, A DÁ, A DÁ
  A PROČ BY NEDALA,
  A DÁ TI DVĚ HUBIČKY
  NA OBĚ TVÁŘIČKY.

TIME: Tick-tock. Yawn.

ŠVEJK returns.

KATY: Well?

ŠVEJK: The Lieutenant has responded to your letter.

KATY: Let me see it.

THE REPLY: On duty till nine p.m. Please make yourself at home. And tell my batman that he is to behave politely, tactfully and satisfy your every whim. I have given him a bottle of wine and a packet of cigarettes. Jindřich.

KATY: Right, soldier, put them in the bedroom.

ŠVEJK: Will you be unpacking them later, madam?

KATY: And open that bottle of wine.

ŠVEJK: Would you like a glass immediately or will I let it breathe?

KATY: Where are those cigarettes?

ŠVEJK: I have them –

KATY: An empty bird cage, what's the point?

ŠVEJK: 'Mission to report –

KATY: Get rid of it.

ŠVEJK: Yes, madam.

KATY: Soldier?

ŠVEJK: Yes, madam?

KATY: Light me up, soldier.

ŠVEJK: ?

KATY: The cigarette –

CAT: ŽUPAJDIJÁ, ŽUPAJDÁ,
   KAŽDÁ HOLKA DÁ!
   A DÁ, A DÁ –

KATY: And what is that dreadful caterwauling?

ŠVEJK: The cat, madam.

KATY: Well put a sock in it.

   ŠVEJK removes his sock puts it in the CAT's mouth.

   Nine p.m., is that what his reply said?

ŠVEJK: 'Mission to report, that is what his letter said.

KATY: And didn't it also say that you are to behave
   politely, tactfully and satisfy my every whim?

ŠVEJK: 'Mission to report, the letter also said that, I
   believe.

KATY: Take off your boots and trousers.

ŠVEJK: Yes, madam –

KATY: I've been travelling all day. I have a lot of whims.

ŠVEJK: 'Mission to report, madam, do you wish me to satisfy them?

ŠVEJK satisfies her. LUKÁŠ enters. He crawls into bed as ŠVEJK crawls out the other side. Soon LUKÁŠ crawls out exhausted and ŠVEJK is hauled back into bed. etc.

ALL: (*Sing.*) A DÁ, A DÁ, A DÁ
A PROČ BY NEDALA,
A DÁ TI DVĚ HUBIČKY
NA OBĚ TVÁŘIČKY.
ŽUPAJDIJÁ, ŽUPAJDÁ,
KAŽDÁ HOLKA DÁ!
A DÁ, A DÁ, A DÁ
A PROČ BY NEDALA.

LOUDHAILER: While the Emperor's armies were cornered in the forests of the Carpathians and rained on day and night by shells which buried whole companies, military strategists met for a council of war –

LUKÁŠ: Well...

TIME: Tick-tock.

ŠVEJK: 'Mission to report, sir... yes?

LUKÁŠ: At ease, Švejk.

ŠVEJK: (*Slumping.*) Thank you, sir.

LUKÁŠ: Have you been polite and respectful to Mistress Katy today?

ŠVEJK: 'Mission to report, Lieutenant Lukáš, repeatedly.

LUKÁŠ: I too. And how are you bearing up to having a mistress about the place?

ŠVEJK: 'Mission to report, Lieutenant Lukáš, sir, I'm fucked.

LUKÁŠ: Yes... I mean, me too... Three weeks!

TIME: Tiiiiiick-toooooock.

LUKÁŠ: How long time has been in passing. Feels like an eternity.

ŠVEJK: War is a cruel mistress.

LUKÁŠ: I'd sooner be in the Carpathians getting my backside blown to smithereens, as I bury my men than burying my... you know.

ŠVEJK: Your man.

LUKÁŠ: Exactly. When will it all be over? Between you and me, I'm beginning to miss my other... lady friends.

ŠVEJK: 'Mission to report sir, if the husband who she's left were to find out where she was – by an anonymous telegram, say – he might come and claim her. A similar thing happened to a friend of mine in Všenory. A woman left her husband and moved in with him. But then again, it was her who sent the anonymous telegram to her husband and when the husband came to claim her he gave my friend such a beating – though he wouldn't in your case since you are an officer – and even if he did, it might be worth a few in the face.

TIME: Tick-tock.

LUKÁŠ: You know Švejk, for a complete idiot, that's not a bad idea.

TIME: Bring-a-ling-a-ling.

KATY: Boys!

ŠVEJK: I'll go send that telegram –

LUKÁŠ: No Švejk, you attend to Mistress Katy. I'll take care of the telegram.

KATY: I said boys –

ŠVEJK: 'Mission to report sir, it's my duty to fetch your personal communications.

LUKÁŠ: Your duty is in the firing line today, soldier.

KATY: One of you! Now!

ŠVEJK: (*Removing trousers.*) 'Mission to report, Madam, I'm coming. Long live Emperor Franz Josef!

LUKÁŠ leaves. ŠVEJK returns to bed.

LOUDHAILER: While the horizons on all battlefields blazed with burning villages and the Empire itself crumbled under the barrage of shells and bullets, for a few soldiers at least the end of this battle was in sight.

LUKÁŠ re-enters with a bottle of champagne that he proceeds to open.

LUKÁŠ: Pleasant enough chap, wasn't he? Did go on a bit about the effect the war was having on his rubber band business... It didn't hurt too much, did it Švejk?

ŠVEJK: (*Emerging with two black eyes.*) 'Mission to report, sir, I have no complaints.

LUKÁŠ: You know, I can't for the life of me work out how he thought that Katy left him for you. (*Pause. Gives ŠVEJK a glass.*) To the good old days!

ŠVEJK: 'Mission to report, the old days.

LUKÁŠ: You know, Švejk, I've been thinking. Perhaps a dog would be a more suitable house guest for a bachelor like myself. And you said you knew a thing or two about dogs.

A park.

VODIČKA: Ha-ha-ha, little soldier boy. You won't find me getting caught up in that racket. Fighting for the Austrians and those filthy Hungarians. I'm telling you,

Švejk, they're not human beings those Hungarians,
they're animals –

ŠVEJK: Any sign yet?

VODIČKA: Bastards. Even the women. Though they know
a thing or too. The women, I mean.

ŠVEJK: Is that her?

VODIČKA: Take it easy, Švejkie, she'll be along. A few
nights back, down in the Vinorhady, there was a
Hungarian bint. Asked her to dance. And what does
the bitch say but no. Says she didn't like the look of
me. So I gave her one in the face and didn't her father
and brother and uncles jump up. Lucky I was with a
few mates from Vršovice. We had to beat up about five
families in the end.

ŠVEJK: What about the dog, Vodička? My Lieutenant –

VODIČKA: Haven't I told you? Everyday at quarter past
the maid comes down by Havlíček Square and in
through the gates, and when she is about exactly where
you are, she lets the Doberman off the lead and sits
approximately where that bench is. In fact, there's the
bitch now. And that's the dog too. Get it? I'll take care
of the animal – you know the routine.

VODIČKA retreats dangling some meat.

MAID: Off you go, Empress, run along and play.

EMPRESS: Bark-bark.

MAID: Don't be long, I've got to get to Ferdinand the
chemist's before it closes.

EMPRESS: Bark-bark.

ŠVEJK: Excuse me Madam, but could you tell me the way to
Žižkov?

MAID: I beg your pardon?

ŠVEJK: Žižkov, I've only recently been transferred to Prague. I'm from the country. You aren't from Prague either, are you.

MAID: No. No I'm not. Empress? I'm sorry, what were you saying?

ŠVEJK: I was enquiring as to where you are from?

MAID: O, Vodňany.

ŠVEJK: Vodňany! How extraordinary. We're practically neighbours.

MAID: Are we? Your face doesn't –

ŠVEJK: I'm from Protovín, originally.

MAID: You are? Then I suppose we are.

ŠVEJK: Fancy that.

EMPRESS: Bark. Bark.

MAID: Protovín? There's a butcher in the square, Pejchar. Do you know him?

ŠVEJK: Know him, he's my brother.

MAID: You aren't one of Jareš' sons?

ŠVEJK: I am indeed.

MAID: Jareš used to deliver beer.

ŠVEJK: Still does, as a matter of fact.

MAID: But he must be over ninety if he's a day.

ŠVEJK: The devil makes work, he always used to say.

MAID: Well, it's been lovely hearing about home, but I really must be moving on. Empress!

ŠVEJK: Yes, yes of course.

MAID: Empress! Where is she?

ŠVEJK: You know what dogs are like. Well, thank you, anyway. I must be pushing on myself.

MAID: But I haven't told you how to get to Žižkov yet.

ŠVEJK: Of course. I am an idiot.

MAID: The number three, from in front of the Castle steps.

ŠVEJK: Number three. Castle steps. Thank you very much.

MAID: Don't mention it. Empress! Empress!

TIME: Ding-ding! All aboard for Žižkov.

VODIČKA emerges with EMPRESS in tow.

EMPRESS: Bark-bark.

VODIČKA: Had to give the bitch the three-day-old liver I was saving for my tea.

EMPRESS: Snarl.

VODIČKA: Shut it or I'll give you one.

ŠVEJK: Here's ten crowns, Vodička. Buy yourself a proper meal.

VODIČKA: Cheers, soldier boy. Have a nice war. You won't see me in that racket, I can tell you.

EMPRESS: Bark?

ŠVEJK: Now, you listen girl, I want to tell you a story. Once upon a time there was a nice little dog called Empress and she lived in a big house with a maid and the Lord knows what else. Then one day a strange man came along and took her away to the army where she became the loyal companion of a Lieutenant and she was given the name of... Temptress. And she never complained or thought about her former life because in the army you leave your past behind you and your thinking to your superiors. Do you understand? And from that day on, Temptress and the Lieutenant and the Lieutenant's batman lived happily ever after. Ruff-ruff? When you think about it, every soldier's been stolen from his home. Ruff?

EMPRESS: Bark.

FOOTNOTE: (*Appears and salutes.*) Footnote. The dog's view of subsequent events. Lieutenant Lukáš comes home from work at the academy and is introduced to his new house guest.

LUKÁŠ: Woof, woof woof, Švejk, woof woof.

ŠVEJK: Ruff-ruff, Ruff, Lukáš, Ruff-ruff Temptress.

LUKÁŠ: (*Delighted.*) Woof, woof woof woof woof woof woof woof, Švejk, woof woof.

ŠVEJK: Ruff ruff ruff, Lukáš, ruff.

LUKÁŠ: Woof?

ŠVEJK: Ruff ruff.

LUKÁŠ: Woof! Temptress! Temptress! Woof woof Temptress.

EMPRESS attempts to copulate with LUKÁŠ' leg.

Woof woof, Švejk!

ŠVEJK: Ruff, ruff ruff, Lukáš.

LUKÁŠ: Woof, Švejk!

ŠVEJK: Ruff, girl, ruff!

ŠVEJK clouts EMPRESS.

FOOTNOTE: Lieutenant Lukáš and the good soldier Švejk take their new friend for a walk.

A park. ŠVEJK and LUKÁŠ walk the dog. They smoke cigars and are the best of friends.

LUKÁŠ: Woof woof woof woof woof woof, Švejk?

FOOTNOTE: Lieutenant Lukáš asks the good soldier about his childhood.

ŠVEJK: (*Growing increasingly upset.*) Ruff ruff ruff ruff ruff ruff ruff ruff ruff ruff ruff ruff ruff ruff ruff ruff ruff ruff ruff ruff ruff ruff ruff –

FOOTNOTE: And Švejk tells his Lieutenant how, when he was only three years old his mother –

LUKÁŠ: (*To FOOTNOTE.*) WOOF, WOOF, Footnote, WOOF!

FOOTNOTE: (*Retreating.*) Yap.

LUKÁŠ: Woof, Švejk.

ŠVEJK: (*Concluding in tears.*) Ruff ruff ruff ruff ruff ruff ruff ruff ruff ruff ruff ruff ruff ruff ruff ruff ruff ruff ruff ruff ruff ruff ruff ruff ruff ruff ruff ruff ruff ruff ruff ruff ruff ruff ruff ruff ruff ruff ruff ruff ruff ruff ruff ruff ruff, Lukáš, ruff.

LUKÁŠ: (*Offering a handkerchief.*) Woof woof, Švejk.

ŠVEJK: Ruff ruff, Lukáš, ruff.

LUKÁŠ: Woof?

ŠVEJK: (*There were happier times.*) Ruff, ruff ruff ruff ruff ruff ruff ruff ruff ruff ruff ruff ruff ruff ruff ruff ruff ruff ruff ruff ruff ruff ruff ruff ruff ruff ruff ruff ruff ruff ruff ruff ruff ruff ruff ruff ruff ruff ruff ruff ruff ruff, Lukáš, ruff.

LUKÁŠ: Ha-ha, Švejk, woof. Woof, woof, Švejk.

GENERAL KRAUS enters.

GENERAL KRAUS: Growl?

LUKÁŠ: Woof? Gulp!

GENERAL KRAUS: Growl growl growl, Lukáš?

LUKÁŠ: Woof, woof woof woof, woof, Kraus, slabber, slabber.

GENERAL KRAUS: Bark. Bark, Kraus.

LUKÁŠ: Woof woof woof woof woof woof Temptress woof woof woof woof woof woof woof woof, Whiiinnne! Woof Kraus.

GENERAL KRAUS: Growl growl growl growl growl growl Temptress! growl growl growl growl growl growl growl growl growl growl growl Empress! Empress growl growl growl growl growl, Lukáš. Bark! bark bark bark Temptress! bark Empress! bark bark bark bark bark bark bark bark bark bark bark bark bark bark bark BARK BARK BARK BARK BARK! Dribble, dribble.

LUKÁŠ: Woof, woof woof, General Kraus. Woof, Švejk, General Kraus.

ŠVEJK: Ruff, Lukáš.

GENERAL KRAUS: BARK, BARK, BARK. Whine, Empress!

EMPRESS: (*Copulating happily with GENERAL KRAUS' leg.*) Daddy, slurp!

GENERAL KRAUS leaves with EMPRESS. Silence.

ŠVEJK: 'Mission to report, sir...

Silence.

Maybe his bark is –

LUKÁŠ: Don't say it, Švejk, don't you dare say it! (*Pause.*) Do you know what you are, Švejk?

ŠVEJK: 'Mission to report, sir, no, I do not.

LUKÁŠ: You are an utter and complete bastard of a bastard's idiot.

ŠVEJK: I am, sir, I am.

LUKÁŠ: Just tell me this, did you steal that dog, Švejk?

ŠVEJK: 'Mission to report, sir, I did not.

LUKÁŠ: Don't lie to me. Did you know that dog was stolen?

ŠVEJK: 'Mission to report, I did know that, sir.

LUKÁŠ: Jesus, Mary and Himmelherrgott, I'll have you shot, you utter and complete bastard of a bastard's idiot. And for once and for all take that stupid look off your face.

ŠVEJK: 'Mission to report, I can't, sir.

LUKÁŠ: Why on earth did you bring me a stolen dog?

ŠVEJK: Because I wanted to make you happy.

LUKÁŠ: And didn't you see the General's notice in the paper?

ŠVEJK: 'Mission to report, I did, sir.

LUKÁŠ: And?

ŠVEJK: And I thought the description bore an uncanny resemblance to Temptress.

LUKÁŠ: Empress, you bastard. Empress!

ŠVEJK: I once knew a fellow called Božetěch who stole dogs from rich people and then, when he saw the notice in the paper, he'd return them and claim the reward.

(*Pause.*) But then, once, he stole this vicious little poodle which chewed everything in his place to pieces, and worse still, long as he waited, the owner didn't put a notice in the paper. So he decided that he'd put a notice in himself saying he'd found this dog and lo and behold this gentleman came and claimed the runt and told Božetěch that he hadn't bothered with a notice since he had no faith in people's honesty but now he saw that there were honest people to be found, his faith was renewed and, as a token of his gratitude, he gave him a book on household plants. Božetěch picked up the poodle and hit the gentleman over the head with it. That was the last time he ever stole a dog. You could say he lost his faith in people too.

Silence.

LUKÁŠ: Do you ever look in a mirror, Švejk?

ŠVEJK: 'Mission to report, I don't if I can help it. I always look a bit lop-sided.

LUKÁŠ: Lop-sided? You're an aberration of nature. How can you live with yourself?

ŠVEJK: With difficulty, sir.

LUKÁŠ: Well, you mightn't have to much longer; General Kraus will probably have the pair of us shot. If we're lucky.

A TRAIN of marching men emerges.

TRAIN: (*Singing.*) THERE ONCE WAS A FINE SOLDIERING MAN WHO GAVE HIS LIFE FOR HIS FATHERLAND –

LUKÁŠ: Permission to report, am here as you ordered in the park yesterday.

Pause.

GENERAL KRAUS: My dog's ruined after being with you. She won't eat anything.

LUKÁŠ: Have you tried three-day-old liver, sir –

GENERAL KRAUS: Have I tried what? I have not. Listen Lukáš, you don't want to make this any worse for you than it already is.

LUKÁŠ: No sir.

GENERAL KRAUS: I've thought, thought for a long time, Lieutenant, about what I should do to prevent a recurrence of this purloining and promenading of dogs belonging to superior officers, and I have decided that you will be transferred forthwith to the 91st Regiment. The high command have informed us that there is a great shortage of officers in the 91st because they have all been killed. You will go directly to Budějovice where they are forming march companies for the Galician front where, with any luck, you will be in the not too distant future. The train for Budějovice departs at six.

GENERAL KRAUS storms out as ŠVEJK enters weighed down with baggage.

TRAIN: (*Singing.*) He did not flinch with mortal fear He faced his death without a tear –

ŠVEJK: 'Mission to report, sir.

LUKÁŠ: We're going to the front, are you happy?

ŠVEJK: 'Mission to report, sir, yes.

LUKÁŠ: Yes?!

ŠVEJK: It will be the greatest day of our lives when we drop down dead for his Imperial Majesty.

TIME: Ding. Ding. Ding. Ding. Ding. Ding. The train for Budějovice departing, platform 6.

TRAIN: (*Singing.*)AND HIS COMRADES COULD NOT HELP BUT CRY,
AS THEY CARRIED HIS BODY SHOULDER HIGH,
AND THE VICTORY MEDAL WAS PINNED TO THE CORPSE
OF THE MAN WHO DIED FOR HIS EMPEROR'S CAUSE.
RATATATAT-RATATATAT-RATATATAT.

*The TRAIN of troops begins to depart. ŠVEJK and LUKÁŠ
are in a compartment.*

ŠVEJK: 'Mission to report, sir, it was only one.

TRAIN: RATATATAT-RATATATAT-RATATATAT.

ŠVEJK: I mean there are so many crooks hanging about
in train stations we should be thankful they didn't
get the lot.

TRAIN: RATATATAT-RATATATAT-RATATATAT.

ŠVEJK: Though I can't see when they got the opportunity
take it. I didn't take my eyes off your luggage from
the minute we left your apartment.

TRAIN: RATATATAT-RATATATAT-RATATATAT.

ŠVEJK: Except when had to go to the little boys' room.

TRAIN: RATATATAT-RATATATAT-RATATATAT.

ŠVEJK: And then I didn't have a kreutzer for the toilet.
And you wouldn't give me a kreutzer because of the
dog business so I had to borrow a kreutzer from a blind
accordionist... And then I had to go back to the toilet...
Maybe they took it then. Just give them half a chance...
Two years ago I read that they robbed a mother of her
pram and her baby was still in it. They left the baby on
the steps of the police station before they pawned the
pram. The mother was arrested for abandoning her
baby. She got two years.

TRAIN: RATATATAT-RATATATAT-RATATATAT.

LUKÁŠ: Will you never have done tormenting me with your accursed stories? It's no use, Švejk, I'm wise to you. I'm never going to speak to you again.

ŠVEJK: Well, rest assured Lieutenant Lukáš, sir, there was nothing important in the suitcase. Just the mirror from the living room, the hat-stand from the hall – and they both belonged to the landlord. And don't worry, Lieutenant Lukáš, I squared it with him, the landlord, I told him we'd return them when we get back from the front. There'll be lots of mirrors and hat-stands in Russia, as soon as we capture a city –

LUKÁŠ: Just, for once, shut up, you drivelling idiot.

ŠVEJK: Yes sir, Lieutenant Lukáš, sir.

TRAIN: Ratatatat-Ratatatat-Ratatatat-Ratatatat.

ŠVEJK: 'Mission to report, Lieutenant Lukáš, sir, but I've often wondered about the emergency cord. Haven't you ever wondered about the emergency cord? I mean, you see emergency cords in every train – and the sign "pull in case of an emergency" – but have you ever seen one work? Do you think they work?... I sometimes wonder if they aren't just for show. To give passengers a false sense of security. You see? I just touched it and nothing. Look, I can put my hand around it and nothing happens. Even if I pull quite hard, I doubt –

TRAIN: SCREECH!

ŠVEJK: 'Mission to report, it does work after all sir.

LUKÁŠ: Švejk!

ŠVEJK: Yes Lieutenant Lukáš, sir?

LUKÁŠ: Why are you ruining my life.

ŠVEJK: Don't worry, sir, it's only a forty crown fine.

LUKÁŠ: Well, I hope you have forty crowns.

ŠVEJK: 'Mission to report, sir, I don't.

LUKÁŠ: Well then, you'll have to walk to Budějovice.
Come on, out you bastard, out and walk – to the front
for all I care.

ŠVEJK: Yes sir, Lieutenant Lukáš, sir. I'll walk.

TRAIN pulls off. ŠVEJK alone. Lights his pipe.

(*Sings.*)AS THE SOLDIERS MARCHED AWAY
THE GIRLS BEGAN TO WEEP.
THEY'D HAVE NO MAN FOR TO LAY
BESIDE, NO, JUST COLD MEMORIES TO KEEP
O, JUST COLD MEMORIES TO KEEP.

Interval.

ACT TWO

GRAMOPHONE: (*Crackle.*) Arma virumque cano – of arms
and the man I sing –
The man, our hero Švejk, who, impelled by fate
Set forth, for fear being late
To join his regiment, the glorious 91st.
And, though fate might hurl her worst
At him, he wavered not in his intent,
But on and on he –

Scratch. Jump.

Like Xenophon, the warrior who, in ancient times,
Found himself deep behind Persian lines
And without compass, map or guide
Still found his way back to the Aegean's side
And cried "Thalassa, Thalassa!"
For deliverance from his Anabasis –

Scratch. Jump.

– So strides throughout the region
To find his Lieutenant and his legion.

OLD WOMAN: Good morning soldier, whither are you
bound?

ŠVEJK: I'm going to my regiment at Budějovice, mother.

OLD WOMAN: Then you're going wrong, soldier. This way
only leads to Klatovy.

ŠVEJK: I believe that a man can get to Budějovice even
from Klatovy.

OLD WOMAN: There's been several like you through
here. One of them walked to Klatovy. A week later the
police were through after him. A week after that he
showed up again in workaday clothes saying he was

home on leave, but the mayor went to the police and that was the end of his leave. He wrote to my niece from the front saying he'd lost both his legs. Take my advice soldier, go by Radomyšl. There's no police there. Here's a potato.

ŠVEJK: Thank you, mother.

OLD WOMAN: God bless.

GRAMOPHONE: He travelled east, he travelled west,
The soldier Švejk he did his best,
Having faith that, since the earth was round,
We all must get to where we're bound
Eventually –

Scratch.

– Putim, Květov and Strakonice
On the road to Budějovice.

A HAYSTACK: Halt, who's there.

ŠVEJK: It's me, Švejk.

A HAYSTACK: What's your regiment? Where are you going?

ŠVEJK: 'Mission to report, the 91st. I'm going to Budějovice.

A HAYSTACK: Why in Christ's name would you be going there?

ŠVEJK: 'Mission to report, my Lieutenant's there.

The HAYSTACK laughs multifariously.

A HAYSTACK: He's going to Budějovice to join his Lieutenant. Do you hear that?

The HAYSTACK laughs harder.

Are you some kind of idiot?

ŠVEJK: Yes, I am.

A HAYSTACK: Listen, we're deserting from the 35th Artillery. We're going to Štěkno. Boruslav has an aunt there. To hell with your Lieutenant, come with us.

GRAMOPHONE: He met deserters from the war.
They counted him one of their score.
But --

Scratch.

-- the earth was round
We all must get to where we're bound
Malčín, Cížová, Putim, Strakonice
On the road to Budějovice.

ANOTHER OLD WOMAN: Whither are you going, soldier?

ŠVEJK: I'm going to Budějovice, mother.

ANOTHER OLD WOMAN: Then you're going wrong, soldier. This way only leads to Putim.

ŠVEJK: I believe that a man can get to Budějovice even from Putim.

ANOTHER OLD WOMAN: There's been several like you through here. They all get rounded up in the end. They write to my niece from the front. They lose limbs. Have you met my niece?

ŠVEJK: I can't say I have, mother.

ANOTHER OLD WOMAN: You'd like her. Take my advice soldier, go by Radomyšl. Here's a potato.

ŠVEJK: Thank you, mother.

ANOTHER OLD WOMAN: God bless.

GRAMOPHONE: He journeyed South, he journeyed North;

The soldier Švejk was good at setting forth
Arriving was the difficulty he found –

Scratch. Jump.

– had being going around – around – around – around –

A HAYSTACK: Halt, who's there.

ŠVEJK: It's me, Švejk.

A HAYSTACK: Where are you going?

ŠVEJK: I'm going to Budějovice.

The HAYSTACK laughs multifariously.

A HAYSTACK: He's going to Budějovice. Do you hear that?

The HAYSTACK laughs harder.

Listen, we're deserting from the 47th Infantry. We're going to Horažd'ovice. Ladislav has an uncle there. Come with us.

GRAMOPHONE: It was not the first time that the thought
Occurred to Švejk that he was caught
In a vicious –

VIRGIN MARY: Where are you going, son?

ŠVEJK: I'm going to Budějovice, Holy Mother.

VIRGIN MARY: You'll never get there this way. This way only leads to Vráž.

ŠVEJK: I believe that a man can get to Budějovice even from Vráž.

VIRGIN MARY: There's been several like you through here. They're all dead. I'd give you a potato, but the soldiers have robbed them all.

ŠVEJK: God bless you –

VIRGIN MARY: Him!

She spits and departs.

GRAMOPHONE: – and wondering how he might go on,
Sat and waited for the light to dawn.

Light breaks through with a choir of ANGELS.

JUDGE: Do you feel alright, Mr Švejk?

ŠVEJK: Yes, your honour, though I fear sleeping in ditches
is not doing my rheumatism any good and I appear to
be having the same old problems.

JUDGE: The vicious circle.

ŠVEJK: Yes, your honour. I don't appear to be able to
break it.

JUDGE: You must examine what you have been doing to
establish what you have been doing wrong.

ŠVEJK: Yes, your honour. But all I am doing is trying to
get to Budějovice.

JUDGE: And what form of navigation are you using?

ŠVEJK: I'm following my instincts.

JUDGE: Then it is your instincts that must be at fault.

ŠVEJK: So to get to Budějovice, I should walk away from
where I think Budějovice is?

JUDGE: That would appear the size of it.

ŠVEJK: Yes, your honour, thank you, your honour.

GRAMOPHONE: So, armed with this fool-proof rationality,
Švejk broke through the vicious circularity
And, by doing his best to avoid his destination,
In no time had concluded his peregrination.

COLONEL SCHRÖDER, Lieutenants LUKÁŠ and KRETSCHMANN.

LOUDHAILER: Meanwhile in the officers' mess at Budějovice. The greatest military minds the Emperor's Forces could muster discussed "The Glorious Licking!"

SCHRÖDER: So tomorrow it is. The glorious licking commences!

KRETSCHMANN: It's a glorious sight alright, sir, the way the men fly out of the trenches and drop like flies in blackcurrant jam. That's how it was in Serbia. "Hurrah!" they shout as they hurl themselves on the enemy; hand grenades primed, bayonets fixed, bullets whistling and buzzing and spitting around the ears. "Hurrah!" shouts another as he jumps up and is blown to pieces on the spot. "Hurrah!" shout his comrades as they cut through the barbed wire only to be stopped dead in their tracks by the cackling kakakakah of the Howitzer. "Hurrah!" shout the enemy. An officer falls. "Hurrah! Hurrah!" shout the men all falling like flies in the blackcurrant jam mud. "Hurrah! Hurrah! Hurrah!" Excuse me, Colonel Schröder, but I think I'm a bit tipsy.

SCHRÖDER: I was thinking more of the glorious licking I intend to get from those Magyar prozzies in Budapest, Kretschmann.

KRETSCHMANN: Yes, Colonel Schröder, sir.

SCHRÖDER: Eh, Lukáš? Can't beat a Hungarian?

LUKÁŠ: No, Colonel Schröder.

SCHRÖDER: Bloody hell, what class of invertebrates are being palmed off on us as officers these days. No juices, no manly juices. I don't know… any sign of that batman of yours yet, Lukáš?

LUKÁŠ: No, Colonel Schröder, sir.

SCHRÖDER: Well, mark him down missing in action.

LUKÁŠ: But we haven't left Bohemia yet.

SCHRÖDER: Bugger it. We're pulling out tomorrow, we don't want to leave our i's undotted and t's uncrossed. This is the army.

LUKÁŠ: No, Colonel Schröder, sir.

SCHRÖDER: So, kill him off. The rivers are high this time of year. Drown him.

KRETSCHMANN: Hurrah! Hurrah!

LUKÁŠ: It will be my pleasure, sir, if only I had known it would be so easy –

ŠVEJK enters.

SCHRÖDER: What's that, Lukáš, seen a ghost?

ŠVEJK: 'Mission to report, sir, I'm back... It's me, Lieutenant Lukáš, 'mission to report.

SCHRÖDER: Who is it, Lukáš?

LUKÁŠ: It's him, sir, it's Švejk.

SCHRÖDER: On the third day he rose. Can't drown a man who was born to be hanged, eh, Lukáš?

LUKÁŠ: Why couldn't you have been just one day later, just one day and you'd have been dead and I could have gone happily off to the front.

ŠVEJK: 'Mission to report, sir, I'm sorry. If I'd known that was your wish I would have arrived tomorrow and been dead –

LUKÁŠ: Well, Švejk, if I can't kill you, I'll place you under regimental arrest for desertion.

ŠVEJK: Yes, sir, but, 'mission to report, I only deserted in order to get back to my regiment.

LUKÁŠ: Don't start, Švejk, just don't start with that rubbish of yours. You know I have always been fair. Firm but fair. Some would say too fair. I could have been promoted long ago if I'd been less fair. But you, you put the most murderous thoughts in my head. How did we live together for so long without me killing you? What would have happened if I had? Nothing. I would have deserved a medal.

ŠVEJK: Yes, Lieutenant Lukáš, you deserve a medal. I remember a captain in our regiment when I was doing my service who shot his wife and he was awarded –

LUKÁŠ: Don't start, I said, Švejk, I don't want to hear you, I just don't want to hear you. Colonel Schröder, I would request you place this man under regimental arrest for desertion.

SCHRÖDER: Come here, soldier.

ŠVEJK: Yes, Colonel Schröder, sir.

SCHRÖDER: Lieutenant Lukáš has told me that you are an idiot, is that so?

ŠVEJK: 'Mission to report, I am, sir.

SCHRÖDER: Well, Lieutenant, according to army custom it is the duty of every officer to educate their own batman. If you chose such an idiot, you must suffer the consequences.

LUKÁŠ: But I didn't choose him, I won him at cards.

SCHRÖDER: I beg your pardon, Lukáš?

LUKÁŠ: I won him at cards...

SCHRÖDER: Do you fancy yourself as some kind of Mephistopheles dicing for human souls?

LUKÁŠ: No sir, Colonel Schröder, sir –

SCHRÖDER: No, Lieutenant, you most certainly are not. I will not tolerate the gambling away of soldiers in my regiment, do you understand? Who would we be left with to fling over the top at the front, if that was the case?

SCHRÖDER roars with laughter. KRETSCHMANN joins in. SCHRÖDER stops abruptly and glares at LUKÁŠ.

LUKÁŠ: Yes, Colonel Schröder, sir.

SCHRÖDER: As for your punishment, Lukáš, you will allow this good soldier to return to his position as your batman and you will treat him with all the respect he deserves as a member of his Majesty's forces. Furthermore, you will undertake to educate him so that we have no more such episodes. Do I make myself clear?

LUKÁŠ: Yes sir, Colonel Schröder, sir.

SCHRÖDER: Now, dismiss.

LUKÁŠ: Yes, sir.

ŠVEJK and LUKÁŠ depart. Pause.

KRETSCHMANN: There's a lot of shitting too. That's another thing. One of my men told me he shitted himself three times. First time when they went over the top with the first "Hurrah!" A second time when they were cutting the wire. And a third when they saw the Russians charging at them shouting "Hurrah! Hurrah!" When they got back to the trenches they found there wasn't one man who hadn't shitted himself.

SCHRÖDER: Tell me Kretschmann, was it in one of these glorious episodes that you lost your leg?

KRETSCHMANN: No, Colonel Schoeder, sir. I was gored by a bull... our supplies had run out.

SCHRÖDER: Eh?

KRETSCHMANN: I grew up in the city... I was trying to milk it.

Train to Hungary. The marching men form a TRAIN.

TRAIN: (*Singing.*) There once was a fine soldiering man
Who gave his life for his fatherland.
He did not flinch with mortal fear
But faced his death without a tear.
And his comrades could not help but cry,
As they carried his body shoulder high
And the victory medal was placed on the corpse
Of the man who died for his Emperor's cause.
Ratatatat-Ratatatat-Ratatatat-Ratatatat-Ratatatat.

In one compartment.

A SOLDIER: Let me out, I can't go on.

DUB: Sit down soldier!

A SOLDIER: I'm not a soldier, I'm a haberdasher.

DUB: That's no excuse.

A SOLDIER: But I don't want to die, Lieutenant Dub, let me off!

DUB: I'm warning you, soldier, you don't know me yet, but if you don't sit down double quick, you'll get to know me.

A SOLDIER: I'm sorry Lieutenant Dub, sir, but –

SOLDIER goes to jump, DUB pulls a gun. SOLDIER jumps. DUB shoots.

In another compartment ŠVEJK enters with a roast chicken and a bottle of wine.

ŠVEJK: 'Mission to report, sir...

LUKÁŠ: (*Miserably.*) ?

ŠVEJK: A roast chicken and a bottle of wine, sir... I thought you might appreciate them... we're still twelve hours from Budapest.

LUKÁŠ: Yes, I would appreciate them.

ŠVEJK: Well, why don't you try some?

LUKÁŠ: Why? Because it is you who's offering them to me, that's why, Švejk.

ŠVEJK: But I am your batman, sir, I'm meant to take care of you.

LUKÁŠ: O, you've taken care of me good and proper alright. I'm the laughing stock of the officers' mess.

ŠVEJK: I certainly never meant to cause you any trouble. If anything happened it was pure coincidence. I only wanted to be helpful, to do something good, it's not my fault that things turn out badly and cause us nothing but misery.

LUKÁŠ: Stop blubbering, please, Švejk. I'll eat your chicken. Just don't blubber.

ŠVEJK: 'Mission to report, all my life, I've only ever tried to do my best –

LUKÁŠ: Švejk, please, I'm eating, so stop. It's good... It's very good.

ŠVEJK: Yes sir, Lieutenant Lukáš, sir... The troops haven't had anything since we left Budějovice. Every time it comes to mealtime, we are given a postcard of his Majesty Franz Josef... They taste a bit like stale communion wafer...

LUKÁŠ: Take this Švejk, and eat it.

ŠVEJK: You're too kind, I couldn't, sir.

LUKÁŠ: Eat, Švejk.

ŠVEJK: If you order me, sir, I suppose I must.

They eat.

LUKÁŠ: You didn't say where you got the chicken. I didn't see any hawkers at the last stop.

ŠVEJK: 'Mission to report, the cook had to take a piss while he was cooking Colonel Schröder's dinner. The thought just occurred to me, it was so unfair, that he'd have this chicken all to himself, while you – !

LUKÁŠ: Švejk!

ŠVEJK: Yes, Lieutenant Lukáš, sir?

LUKÁŠ: You didn't tell me that, Švejk. That too is an order.

They continue eating.

TRAIN: (*Singing.*) HE STOOD STEADFAST BY HIS MORTAR GUN,
HE STOOD STEADFAST AND HE BLASTED ON.
HE STOOD STEADFAST AS IT RAINED WITH BOMBS
AND HE STOOD STEADFAST WITHOUT HIS ARMS.
RATATATAT-RATATATAT-RATATATAT-RATATATAT-RATATATAT-RATATATAT.

TIME: Budapest!

TRAIN: RATATATAT-RATATATAT-PSSSSSSSSSSSSSSSSSSST!!!!

DUB finds a soldier in bed with a PROSTITUTE.

DUB: Thought you'd grab a bit of r and r with a Hungarian whore, eh, soldier?

SOLDIER: Lieutenant Dub, sir.

DUB: Don't you Lieutenant Dub me. You might think you know me soldier, but you don't know me yet. You don't know my bad side. Do you want to see my bad side?

SOLDIER: What, Lieutenant Dub? No –

DUB shoots the SOLDIER.

DUB: Perhaps you'll know me a little better next time –

PROSTITUTE: You've killed him.

DUB shoots the PROSTITUTE.

DUB: Don't interrupt me you... naughty, naughty little girl...

As the PROSTITUTE flops forward, DUB is aroused. DUB takes off his jacket and snuggles up beside her.

Mmmmmmm! Mummy!

LUKÁŠ's quarters. LUKÁŠ enters as ŠVEJK is cleaning his boots.

LUKÁŠ: (*Drunk.*) It's a most important matter, Švejk.

ŠVEJK: Yes, Lieutenant Lukáš, sir.

LUKÁŠ: Top secret. The need for caution cannot be overstated.

ŠVEJK: I will not overstate it, sir.

LUKÁŠ: Don't... don't start confusing me, Švejk. Here is a letter. The lady is called Mrs Etelka Kákonyi. She lives at 16 Sopron Street. Do you know Budapest?

ŠVEJK: 'Mission to report, sir, no, I don't have a bald pig's clue.

LUKÁŠ: I'll draw you a map... First thing tomorrow, without fail, deliver the letter to her and her alone, and wait for an answer. I'm depending on you.

ŠVEJK: 'Mission to report, you can depend on me, sir.

THE LETTER: Dear Madam, tonight at the theatre, I was present at the play which upset you so much. I watched you during the whole of the first act. It seemed to me that your husband enjoyed the foul spectacle on offer –

LUKÁŠ: Do you know, when they did their high kicks, Švejk, you could see that they shave themselves, these women, like Tartars, Švejk, it's simply...

THE LETTER: But you, Madam, were disgusted by it. This was not art, but the denigration of the most sensitive human things –

LUKÁŠ: And the breasts, Švejk, she had the most capital breasts.

THE LETTER: Excuse me for writing to you so candidly, but no woman I have ever seen has made such an impression on me as you have. As for your husband, he is doubtless a complete boor. I do not wish to upset your domestic tranquillity and my only desire is to talk to you, privately, about art. Yours –

LUKÁŠ: Excuse me, Švejk.

LUKÁŠ exits weeping. ŠVEJK and VODIČKA are walking in the street, sharing a hip flask. A DRUNKEN HUNGARIAN SOLDIER looks on disinterestedly.

VODIČKA: (*In the uniform of the Engineers.*) Ha-ha-ha, little soldier boy, fancy meeting you here. Off to the front, are you? You won't find me caught up in that racket. Getting myself killed for these Hungarian bastards! The Engineers is the life for me. Digging the trenches for you poor bastards to be buried in.

ŠVEJK: Vodička, I'd love to stop and chat, but I have to deliver a letter –

VODIČKA: To a Hungarian? That's the problem with Budapest, nice enough place, but it's full of the bastards. Wait till I tell you, when I first came here we had to sit in this classroom while these tosspots explained to us what drainage ditches were. Drainage ditches! I ask you. I didn't wheedle out of serving at the front to listen to this shite. So that afternoon I come straight down here to Sopron Street with one thing on my mind; find a nice little pub, get ghee-eyed, slap a few Hungarians and crawl home –

They arrive at the door.

ŠVEJK: Number 16. You wait here, I'll drop the letter up and be back in a minute.

VODIČKA: What? Do you think I'd leave my old flower Švejkie brave a posse of Magyar bastards on his own? Listen, I'll go up with you and if he gets a bit lippy, I'll give him a few in the face.

ŠVEJK: It's a she. (*Pause. VODIČKA can't take a hint.*) Listen, then... if you're coming –

VODIČKA: No better man. I'll risk it for a biscuit.

VODIČKA knocks at the door. A hand comes out. VODIČKA takes the letter from ŠVEJK and hands it in. Door closes.

Anyway, like I was telling you, I found this nice quiet place. Just two old lads nattering away in Hungarian. And the funny thing is, the more pissed I got, the more angry I got – the sound of Hungarian gets to you after a while. But I must have been more pissed than I realised because I didn't notice that eight Hussars had gone into the restaurant part, so when the time came to give the old boys their slapping, the Hussars jumped in and –

Door opens and MR KÁKONYI emerges with his napkin still around his neck.

MR KÁKONYI: Baszom az anyát, baszom az istenet, baszom a Kristus Máriát, baszom as astyádot, baszom a Világot!

FOOTNOTE: (*Appears and salutes.*) Footnote: a string of obscene Hungarian oaths. Literally "Fuck your mother, God, Christ, the Virgin Mary and all the world" –

MR KÁKONYI: What the hell is the meaning of this? Where's the swine who brought me this filth, I'll –

VODIČKA: Steady now, Mister, if you know what's good for you. My friend here brought you this letter, but talk to him politely or I'll –

ŠVEJK: We can see you were having dinner, we didn't want to disturb you –

VODIČKA: Don't demean yourself.

MR KÁKONYI: Baszom az anyát, baszom az istenet, baszom a Kristus Máriát –

FOOTNOTE: A string of obscene –

VODIČKA: We get the idea, runt!

MR KÁKONYI: I will write to the regimental commander, I'll write to the Ministry of War, I'll write to the papers –

ŠVEJK: Sir, it's me who wrote the letter. Not the Lieutenant. The signature and the name are false. I like your wife very much. Very tasty. Ich liebe Ihre Frau. I'm up to my tonsils in love with her. She's capital. And her diddies –

MR KÁKONYI tries to thump ŠVEJK, VODIČKA trips him, drags him around the stage, starts beating him. The DRUNKEN HUNGARIAN SOLDIER is hit by a mis-thrown punch and gets drawn into the fight. FOOTNOTE too is soon drawn in. The scene of mass violence continues in elegant slow motion to the sound of 'The Trumpet Shall Sound' from Handel's <u>Messiah</u>. Crescendo.

TIME: Bring-a-ling-aling.

The brawlers are hauled off by TWO MILITARY POLICE. Diminuendo. Parallel scenes between SCHRÖDER and LUKÁŠ on one side; ŠVEJK and an ARMY INTELLIGENCE OFFICER on the other.

SCHRÖDER: (*Reading from a newspaper.*) "Lieutenant Jindřich Lukáš, the notorious Czech philanderer, proceeded to rape Mrs Kákonyi in her own dining-room during lunch in the presence of her husband whom he had threatened with a sword and forced to gag his own wife's mouth with a towel to prevent her screaming." (*Pause.*) I must say, Lukáš, you've certainly started some palaver with your old swagger stick, eh? You old snake in the grass. In the mess we always took you for a – you know – for a queer chappie. Divisional court-martial are up in arms, of course. They want your balls on a platter. But they're a bunch of Hungarian bastards. And as for this Švejk of yours –

ŠVEJK and INTELLIGENCE OFFICER.

ARMY INTELLIGENCE OFFICER: Whose writing is this, soldier?

ŠVEJK: 'Mission to report, sir, it's mine.

ARMY INTELLIGENCE OFFICER: Do you think I'm an idiot, soldier?

ŠVEJK: 'Mission to report, sir, I do not. You must be intelligent to be an intelligence officer.

ARMY INTELLIGENCE OFFICER: Don't be smart.

ŠVEJK: I like Mrs Kákonyi very much. Very tasty. I'm up to my tonsils in love with her. She has capital diddies –

ARMY INTELLIGENCE OFFICER: Enough of your lip, sonny Jim. I want you to copy the letter you have in your hand, word for word, so we can compare... where is the letter, soldier?

ŠVEJK: (*Chewing the letter.*) 'Mission to report, we've been locked in the garrison gaol for three days, sir, we've had no rations.

ARMY INTELLIGENCE OFFICER: You devious little... I'll see you hanged, I will...

LUKÁŠ and SCHRÖDER.

SCHRÖDER: Lukáš, just between you and me, how many times did you bag Mrs Kákonyi? Just a rough figure. Don't try and pretend you'd only started to correspond. A few years back I spent three weeks in Erlau. Bedded a different Hungarian woman every day for three weeks. Young ones, married ones, old ones. I drilled them so thoroughly that when I got back to my regiment I could hardly walk –

ŠVEJK and VODIČKA in prison.

VODIČKA: Do you know what he asked me, Švejkie? Do you know what the intelligence bastard asked me? He asked me if I was a Slavophile. A Slavophile, I ask you! How can I be a Slavophile when I don't know what the Jaysus it is.

ŠVEJK: Listen Vodička, the best thing you can do is just pretend to be an idiot.

VODIČKA: I'm not going to pretend to be an idiot for no one.

Switch to LUKÁŠ and SCHRÖDER.

SCHRÖDER: Of course, I believe Švejk is just a pawn in a systematic agitation against Bohemian military units in transit through Hungary. And the fellow must have character after all. The trick he pulled off with that letter. I like the bastard. But to avoid proceedings, we must get you out of Budapest. Yourself and Švejk are to be assigned to Captain Ságner's eleventh march company. I'm promoting Švejk to company orderly. You leave for Galicia tonight.

LUKÁŠ: Orderly? Colonel Schröder, sir! You don't know what you do –

Silence. Switch to VODIČKA and ŠVEJK leaving prison.

VODIČKA: Off to the front, Švejkie? You won't catch me in that racket.

ŠVEJK: Listen, Vodička, when the war's over, come see me. Palivec's at Na Bojišti. From six o'clock every day.

VODIČKA: What's it like there?

ŠVEJK: You'd like it. They've got Velkopopovický.

VODIČKA: That piss!

ŠVEJK: Well, there's girls too. Sometimes.

VODIČKA: Well just make sure there's some the night I stop by.

ŠVEJK: I'll make sure.

VODIČKA: Right then, you're on, six o'clock after the war.

TIME: Ding. Ding. Ding. Ding. Ding –

ŠVEJK: Better make it half six, in case I'm held up.

VODIČKA waves good-bye as LUKÁŠ enters gloomily.

TIME: Ding.

ŠVEJK: 'Mission to report, I'm back again.

TIME: Tick-Tock.

ŠVEJK: Lieutenant Lukáš, it's me, sir. Colonel Schröder swore at me a bit, but he recognised my innocence and he told me to report to you as company orderly in charge of all our supplies... Lieutenant Lukáš, sir?

TIME: Tick –

LUKÁŠ: We're lost.

TIME: Tock. Train for Eastern Galicia now departing platform six! 11th march company of the 91st Regiment board –

TRAIN: (*Singing.*) AND HIS COMRADES COULD NOT HELP BUT CRY, AS THEY CARRIED HIS BODY SHOULDER HIGH.
AND THE VICTORY MEDAL WAS PLACED ON THE CORPSE
OF THE MAN WHO DIED FOR HIS EMPEROR'S CAUSE.
RATATATAT-RATATATAT-RATATATAT-RATATATAT-RATATATAT-RATATATAT.

LUKÁŠ, DUB and SÁGNER in one compartment, COOK, ŠVEJK and MAREK in the second. Compartment one.

SÁGNER: "The Sins of Our Fathers", a novel by Ludwig Ganghofer, turn to page 161 and commit to memory.

Compartment two.

COOK: (*Drinking sherry.*) Postcards? How am I expected to feed a thousand men day after day with postcards?

ŠVEJK: They are postcards of his Majesty Franz Josef.

COOK: That does not make them more nutritious. I used to cook at the Hapsburg. I know about the transmigration of the soul.

MAREK: Speaking of which, how do you want to die?

COOK: What do you mean? I want to cook. What kind of question is that to ask a cook? Who do you think you are?

MAREK: Volunteer Marek. Since I once worked as a newsboy I have been appointed company historian and have been instructed to record our company's valiant deeds in battle. I thought I'd write up a few of our deaths before we get too busy. We'll be remembered as the most heroic company in the entire Austro-Hungarian Landwehr. The telegraph operator was quite delighted with his fate. He went down having defended his telegraph machine from twelve marauding Cossacks with nothing but a pencil stub and a ham sandwich. So, what's it to be?

COOK: I know about the transmigration of souls. I don't want to die.

ŠVEJK: I've read about the transmigration of souls. A few years back I decided to educate myself because I didn't want to get left behind. I went to the Industrial reading room in Prague. But, because I had holes in my trousers, they thought I was there to steal the coats, so they threw me out. But they were in such a hurry that they forgot to take the book from me that I'd picked up. It was on the transmigration of souls. It sounded reasonable enough in theory. But when there's a war on transmigrating must get very complicated indeed. How many changes must a soul go through before it becomes an infantryman, or an orderly, or a cook? Then, before it can get used to its new body, the body gets blown to pieces by a shell and the soul goes into a horse in the cavalry, and when this horse gets blown to bits by another shell, the soul moves on to a cow who's standing in the next field watching the action, and when the fighting stops, the starving battle weary troops see the cow and kill it and make goulash out of it and he's back in the soul of the soldiers...

COOK: I once worked at the Hapsburg. Now I am the butt of an idiot's jokes.

*Compartment one. DUB shoots a PEASANT by whom
the TRAIN is passing. ALL look up momentarily then
return to what they were doing. Compartment two.*

ŠVEJK: What fate do you have in mind for me, Marek?

MAREK: You're a difficult case, Švejk, I'll have to dream
up a special fate for you.

ŠVEJK: What paper did you work for?

MAREK: The Animal World. Do you know it?

ŠVEJK: It was my favourite. It's a very informative
magazine. I knew a journalist who wrote for it. Hašek.
There was hardly a week when he didn't announce the
discovery of some miraculous new beast. The Sulphuric
Stomached Whale –

MAREK: It was the size of a large halibut and had a belly
full of acid which it used to spit at its prey to stun them.

ŠVEJK: And the Cantankerous Kenyan Cat.

MAREK: A moggy who lived on the top of Mount
Kilimanjaro.

ŠVEJK: Hašek seemed to have all the wonders of the world
to hand.

MAREK: He made it all up. He said people were bored
with workaday cats and dogs and canaries.

ŠVEJK: What a pity. So there is nothing in the world that is
not already known.

MAREK: Wouldn't seem so.

Compartment one.

SÁGNER: Right then gentlemen, p.161 of "The Sins of
Our Fathers", volume two. Have you all memorised it?

DUB: Yes sir, Captain Ságner. There's a woman called Martha who has taken a play she is writing out of her desk and wonders aloud whether the public feels any sympathy with the hero. Albert appears to think not. Martha feels disappointed, she burns the play –

SÁGNER: That's as maybe, but the relative merits of Martha's literary activities are not what concern us at present, Dub. This, gentlemen, is strictly confidential information. Why is this strictly confidential information? I'll tell you why, because this is the new, foolproof key to deciphering telegrams.

DUB: Would that be the Archduke Albrecht Code?

SÁGNER: Yes, Dub. Now if I may continue. Say, for example –

LUKÁŠ: Permission to report, sir –

SÁGNER: What is it Lukáš?

LUKÁŠ: We appear to have been issued with volume one.

SÁGNER: What? But I ordered volume two. I distinctly ordered the orderly –

Compartment two.

LUKÁŠ: Švejk!

ŠVEJK: Yes sir, Lieutenant Lukáš, sir.

LUKÁŠ: This book.

ŠVEJK: "The Sins of Our Fathers" as ordered, sir.

LUKÁŠ: This is volume one, Švejk.

ŠVEJK: 'Mission to report, sir, I don't know very much about books, sir. I only ever knew one writer. We were just talking about him. He used to read his stories at

Mr Palivec's. They were very sad stories and everyone used to roar with laughter at them. He'd weep and pay for everyone's drink and...Yes, sir, anyway, sir, I went to the regimental office and the quartermaster sergeant showed me the books and we did have a laugh. You see the books were in two parts, volume one and volume two and, like I said, I don't know very much about books, but I do know you don't start a book from the second part, Lieutenant Lukáš, sir –

LUKÁŠ: Those books were not for reading, Švejk.

ŠVEJK: You see, I mustn't know much about books –

LUKÁŠ: I'm telling you, I'm telling you Švejk, this is the last, the very last... We're lost, Švejk, do you realise? We are up to our teeth in shit without a paddle or a prayer –

SÁGNER: Piss-break!

TRAIN: Pssssssssst!

TRAIN breaks up. MEN piss against the wall. ŠVEJK steals away. LUKÁŠ is left alone at the front of the stage.

LUKÁŠ: Maybe it's me. Maybe this is how it really is. Maybe all these pock marked hills, burnt out houses, black leafless trees, maybe all these bits and pieces of flesh and bone and scraps of uniforms swimming in the shit and mud, maybe all this is normal. Maybe it's me. Maybe I'm mad. Christ! We are lost.

ŠVEJK enters with a bottle of cognac. He is about to give it to LUKÁŠ.

LUKÁŠ: To hell with it, to hell with it all. I need a piss.

LUKÁŠ goes to the wall to piss at the same moment as DUB intercepts ŠVEJK.

DUB: You. Yes, you, I know you. Where have you been?

ŠVEJK: 'Mission to report, buying sweets. Would you like one? I've already tasted them, they taste like blackcurrant jam –

DUB: Don't you know who I am, soldier?

ŠVEJK: Yes, sir, you're Lieutenant Dub, sir.

DUB: That might be my name, but do you really know me? My bad side?

ŠVEJK: 'Mission to report, no, sir.

DUB: Then what's that under your tunic, soldier?

ŠVEJK produces bottle of cognac.

ŠVEJK: 'Mission to report, it's some drinking water I pumped into an empty bottle of cognac. I still have a terrible thirst after the postcard supreme. I think Cook oversalted it –

DUB: Tell me then, soldier, if this is water, why is this water yellow?

ŠVEJK: I think there must be some iron in it.

DUB: Well, a little iron never did anyone any harm. Why don't you go ahead and quench that thirst of yours then, soldier? Drink it, drink it all down in one draught.

ŠVEJK: Yes sir, Lieutenant Dub, sir. Glug, glug –

DUB: It will be a miracle if I don't get the better of you. Here, that's enough, give it –

ŠVEJK: Glug, glug. (*Finished.*) 'Mission to report, sir, there was an awful lot of iron in it.

DUB: I'll give you iron. Where'd you get that water, soldier? You got it from a hawker. It wasn't water, it was cognac, soldier!

ŠVEJK: 'Mission to report, I got it from that rusty pump where those dogs have been –

DUB: Let me taste it then.

THE PUMP: Eeeep Eeeep Eeeep –

DUB: Glug, glug, glug

ŠVEJK: – pissing, Lieutenant Dub, and shitting...

DUB: You! You don't know me yet, soldier, you don't know how bad my bad side can be, you'll get to know me soon enough, you bastard, I'm telling you. Drop that bottle and drill, soldier.

DUB fires at ŠVEJK's feet.

ŠVEJK: Yes, sir, Lieutenant Dub, sir.

DUB: Attention! Eyes right! Eyes Left! Right turn! Left turn! As you were! Attention! Right incline! Left incline! Fix bayonet! Unfix bayonet! Prepare for prayer! Kneel for prayer! Finish prayer! Target piss wall! Ready! Aim!

DUB'S INNARDS: We've been hit! Repeat. We've been hit!

DUB: Maintain aim! What was that?

DUB'S INNARDS: We're going down!

ŠVEJK: 'Mission to report, sir, it sounded like your innards.

DUB: Shut up! Shut up!

DUB doubles up.

DUB'S INNARDS: Abandon ship! Repeat; abandon –

DUB starts to dissolve.

ŠVEJK: 'Mission to report, am maintaining aim and awaiting further instructions, Lieutenant Dub, sir.

(*Pause. ŠVEJK examines rifle butt.*) 4268. It's the same number on this rifle butt as there was on a railway engine in Pečky on track 16. Isn't that a coincidence, Lieutenant Dub? They were to take it away to Lysá nad Labem for repairs but the engine driver wasn't good with figures. The stationmaster called him into his room and said to him "There's an engine no. 4268 needs taking away for repairs. Now I know you and figures and if I write it down, you'll only lose the piece of paper, so I'll show you an easy way of remembering the number. Listen, the number of the engine you have to take for repairs in Lysá nad Labem is 4268. The first number is 4, the second is 2. 4 divided by 2 makes 2 and so you get 42. Then multiply 4 by 2 and you get 8 which is the last number. So already you know that the first number is 4, the second 2 and the fourth 8. All that has to be done is to remember that the third, which is twice 3, is 6. And that's it. So now you've got it fixed in your mind. And there is, of course, an easier way –

DUB: (*Whispering.*) Water!

ŠVEJK: 'Mission to report, didn't quite catch that, am maintaining aim and awaiting further instructions, Lieutenant Dub, sir... Well, then the stationmaster went on; "8 minus 2 is 6," he explained, "So you already have 68. 6 minus 2 is 4. So now you have the 4, the 6 and the 8 and only the 2 has to be inserted. 4268. And, in fact," he went on, "there's yet another way of doing it by multiplication and division. Remember that twice 42 is 84. There's twelve months to a year. So subtract 12 from 84 and you have 72. Take another 12 away from that and you have 60. Keep the 6 and cross out the 0. Now we have 42, 68, 4. When you cross out the 0 you can also cross out the last 4 and again we get the number of the engine." ... 'Mission to report, am maintaining aim and –

ŠVEJK's gun goes off.

'Mission to report, Lieutenant Dub, the gun appears to have gone off. Should I maintain position?

LUKÁŠ stops pissing and arrives at the scene. There is a hole in his hat.

LUKÁŠ: What now, Švejk?

ŠVEJK: 'Mission to report, Lieutenant Lukáš, sir, Lieutenant Dub told me to maintain position while I was doing punishment drill because I had gone to get you some cognac from one of the hawkers because you seemed a bit lowly and I thought it would cheer you up but Lieutenant Dub caught me and thought I was buying it for myself and when I told him it was water he ordered me to drink it and then he asked me where I got it and I told him I got it from that rusty old pump where the mangy dogs were pissing and shitting, and I don't think he's very well and 'mission to report I don't feel very well because I think the cognac is starting to have an effect. I only wanted to cheer you up.

ŠVEJK falls on DUB.

ANGELIC CHOIR OF SOLDIERS: (*Singing.*)
COME GATHER ROUND THE EMPEROR'S FLAG,
SOLDIERS, COMRADES, BROTHERS ALL.
SAY YOUR GOOD-BYES AND PACK YOUR BAGS
SOLDIERS, COMRADES, BROTHERS ALL.
TIS TIME TO FIGHT THE ENEMY
SOLDIERS, COMRADES, BROTHERS ALL.
TIS TIME TO DIE FOR YOU AND ME,
SOLDIERS, COMRADES, BROTHERS ALL.

MAREK and DUB in a car.

DUB: You, Marek, isn't it? Where are we going, Marek?

MAREK: This is the only road left, Lieutenant Dub, sir.

DUB: But there are shells raining down on all sides.

MAREK: Didn't you hear, Lieutenant Dub, there's a war on.

A white light.

DUB: What was that? We're flying.

MAREK: A detour, sir.

DUB: And – Christ! – the road's all soft and creamy. Where are we, soldier?

MAREK: The Milky Way. That's Venus underneath us.

DUB: What is the meaning of this?

MAREK: This is your fate, Lieutenant Dub, sir.

DUB: My fate? Who are you to know my fate?

MAREK: I'm company historian, sir.

DUB: But where does this road lead?

MAREK: To heaven, sir.

A queue of WAR WOUNDED forms.

DUB: And these soldiers! Why has that soldier got no head? It's in the rulebook; all soldiers must have heads.

MAREK: We are at the gates, Lieutenant Dub, sir. I must be getting back. I've yet to determine a fate for over half our company.

DUB: You can't leave me here, on my own. Don't you know who I am?

MAREK is gone. An ANGELIC CHOIR sing the 'Hallelujah' chorus from Handel's <u>Messiah</u>.

ST PETER: (*As a colonel.*) Open your ugly mugs wider,

you bastards. Is that any way to sing the Hallelujah Chorus? You swine want to stay in purgatory forever? Let's do it again and put some soul into it this time.

ANGELIC CHOIR OF SOLDIERS: Hallelujah!

DUB: I request to be taken to the Imperial Royal Headquarters of the Lord, Colonel St Peter, sir.

ST PETER: And who do you think you are?

DUB: You don't know me? I ... I am Lieutenant Dub, St Peter, sir.

ST PETER: Dub? I'm afraid you'll have to do better than that. You've got to be someone here, in heaven. Take him to the cholera unit.

The TROOPS, still singing, begin to escort him away.

DUB: Cholera? But I don't have cholera! –

LOUDHAILER: The Galician frontier! Forward March! Forward March, you bastards!

The SOLDIERS form two columns of men. They march grimly forward. Fleeing in the opposite direction are GALICIAN PEASANTS – farmers, mothers, wives with babies, hawkers – they carry what few possessions they have – chickens, a gramophone, a loudhailer, a bottle of cognac. LUKÁŠ rides a horse beside the column. He keeps pace with ŠVEJK who carries his bag.

ŠVEJK: – it's a great advantage for the farmers, when their fields are covered with the dust of an entire regiment, Lieutenant Lukáš. When I was doing my national service, there was a Lieutenant called Vaněk. When the soldiers used to complain that their rations were inedible he'd say: "What do you think this is? A delicatessen? In time of war the soil in which you'll be buried will not complain about you, nor will it care what you ate before you died. The earth will decompose you and gobble you up, boots and all. But don't worry, men, nothing ever disappears entirely. Out of the earth you're buried in, there'll grow corn for bread for new soldiers who'll complain about their rations and then die and then fertilise the land afresh." That's what he used to say. Are you still upset about the little misunderstanding in Budapest? Or about Lieutenant Dub? I really didn't mean for him to get cholera from that rusty pump.

Pause.

LUKÁŠ: I don't give a kreutzer for Dub. He was a shit. He had it coming. And you didn't give him cholera. He got the cholera because the doctor mis-diagnosed his dysentery as cholera and sent him to a cholera clinic, where he got cholera.

ŠVEJK: That's good, sir. I wouldn't want that on my conscience. 'Mission to report then, sir, why are you upset?

LUKÁŠ: Are you blind? Look around you... Look at the valley, gored from one side to the other –

ŠVEJK: 'Mission to report, it's as though an army of giant moles had been digging all night... And look, there, in that tree, Lieutenant Lukáš, sir, there's an Austrian boot. There's a shinbone still in it.

LUKÁŠ: Field upon field of nameless white crosses on devastated hills.

ŠVEJK: It's a bit different to Prague, alright.

LUKÁŠ: What kind of an idiot are you? No, don't answer that. Tell me one of your stories, Švejk.

ŠVEJK: Are you sure, sir?

LUKÁŠ: Yes, Švejk, please.

ŠVEJK: Well, I know a short one about a postmistress from Milevsko. I was thinking of her only a moment ago when you ordered me to look around, though I can't for the life of me think why I thought of her.

LUKÁŠ: Švejk, you're talking tripe again.

ŠVEJK: 'Mission to report, I am, sir. The story really is awful tripe. In fact I've no idea how anything so tripe-ish could have come into my head. It must be my natural idiocy. At the last stop the cook fell down drunk in a ditch after drinking the last bottle of cooking sherry. He shouted from the ditch "man is destined to know the truth that he may with his spirit rule the universe in harmony." When we tried to lift him out he scratched and bit like a wildcat –

LUKÁŠ: But what about this damned postmistress?

ŠVEJK: 'Mission to report, sir, I'm sorry, I was forgetting her. She was a good woman and carried out her duties at the post office, but she was under the delusion that everyone was persecuting her. So, every evening she would close the post office and go straight to the police with a list of everyone who had persecuted her that day. Her main persecutor was the parish priest who, she claimed, had indecent intentions towards her but the sergeant knew that the said priest had indecent intentions towards his niece and so told the postmistress to bugger off and stop annoying him. So she, the silly cow, denounced the sergeant for aiding and abetting the priest in his indecent intentions towards her. A medical board examined her and they concluded that she was completely off her trolley and she was deemed unfit for a position in the state service.

LUKÁŠ: Jesus, Švejk, that is the worst story I have ever heard.

ŠVEJK: 'Mission to report, I know, I warned you it was awful tripe.

LUKÁŠ: You let pearls of wisdom fall through your hands like water through a sieve.

ŠVEJK: Not every man can have wisdom, sir. Stupid people have to exist too. If everyone was wise, there'd be so much good sense in the world that we'd all be driven crazy by it.

LUKÁŠ: Why do I feel the need to talk to you, Švejk? You'd think by now I'd know better.

ŠVEJK: 'Mission to report, Lieutenant Lukáš, sir, it's a question of habit. It's due to the fact that we've known each other so long and that we've gone through so much together. And if we got into trouble together, it was only ever bad luck. I wish nothing better for myself than to be of help to you.

Pause.

LUKÁŠ: Aren't you afraid, Švejk?

ŠVEJK: Afraid of what, sir?

LUKÁŠ: This, Švejk.

ŠVEJK: Like I said, sir, it's a bit different to Prague, sir.

LUKÁŠ: A bit different! It's a nightmare. A shambles. It's the end of the world.

ŠVEJK: Is it, sir?

LUKÁŠ: Maybe you're not such an idiot after all –

ŠVEJK: O, 'mission to report, I am, sir –

LUKÁŠ: Maybe it's your way of surviving – all this – hear no evil, see no evil.

ŠVEJK: If truth be told, sir, I'm not sure how I survive at all.

LUKÁŠ: Have you ever been in love, Švejk?

ŠVEJK: 'Mission to report, there was a woman, sir.

LUKÁŠ: Did you love her? Did she love you?

ŠVEJK: It was when I was doing my national service. She wrote me a letter once. I have it here. I keep it with me all the time.

LUKÁŠ: Let's hear it then, Švejk.

THE LETTER: You bloody bastard. You bloody, bloody bastard. Corporal Kříž came to Prague on leave. I danced with him at U Kocanů and he told me he had seen you at the Happy Frog with some tart. It's all over between us. Your ex, Božena. P.S. Corporal Kříž knows a thing or two, I can tell you, and he's going to bash your face in when he gets back to camp because I asked him to, you bloody bastard.

Pause.

LUKÁŠ: I'm frightened, Švejk.

ŠVEJK: I am your batman, sir, I'll look after you.

> (*SINGS.*) AT THE DARKEST HOUR OF NIGHT
> WHEN ALL THE WORLD IS SLEEPING TIGHT
> MY LOVE WHISPERS IN MY EAR
> TIS TIME TO PUT OFF ALL YOUR FEARS.
>> HOLD ME,
>> HOLD ME –

LUKÁŠ: Look at me, Švejk.

ŠVEJK: Yes, sir, Lieutenant Lukáš, sir.

LUKÁŠ: For once and for all, won't you take that idiotic look off your face, Švejk?

ŠVEJK: 'Mission to report, sir, no, I won't.

CHORUS OF SOLDIERS: (*Singing.*) AND IN A WARM EMBRACE,
WHEN SHE KISSES MY WET FACE,
THE NIGHT CAN'T SEE MY TEARS.
TIS TIME TO PUT OFF ALL YOUR FEARS.
    HOLD ME,
    HOLD ME
AT THE DARKEST HOUR OF NIGHT
WHEN ALL THE WORLD IS SLEEPING TIGHT –

As the song continues the stage darkens and fills with smoke. The sound of gun-fire, shells exploding, shouts, yells and roars, rises. The singing is soon submerged by the sound of the tumult. Then, diminuendo. Out of the mist emerges ŠVEJK.

ŠVEJK: 'Mission to report, Lieutenant Lukáš, sir, I'm here. Lieutenant Lukáš, sir? There was some noise and some smoke and I lost sight of you and didn't see what happened to you... Lieutenant Lukáš, sir, it's me, Švejk. Where are you, sir?

ANGELIC CHOIR. The JUDGE appears.

Long live Emperor Franz Josef, your honour.

JUDGE: Do you feel alright, Mr Švejk?

ŠVEJK: Yes, your honour, my rheumatism's been better the last while.

JUDGE: That's good.

ŠVEJK: But I've lost my Lieutenant. And I said I'd look out for him. He hasn't been himself lately.

JUDGE: Few have. Even you.

ŠVEJK: 'Mission to report, your honour, I am always myself, unfortunately.

JUDGE: Well officially speaking I'm afraid to say you are yourself no more. Marek's history of the company. You were crucified as a traitor three days ago. Sorry to be the bearer of bad news.

ŠVEJK: Marek did say he had something special in mind. But a traitor? Me?

JUDGE: According to Marek, you came upon a company of Russians while out on reconnaissance. You managed to outwit the lot of them by appearing to surrender and then marching with them into a field of their own landmines where they were all blown sky high. Unfortunately your uniform was burnt to shreds by the blast so you put on one of the dead Russians' uniforms and were soon arrested by an Austrian company who, when they found out you were really a Czech in a Russian uniform, crucified you as a traitor. The Austrian battalions are not especially fond of Czechs.

ŠVEJK: So it would seem. It is quite an unfortunate fate. Though I can't say it surprises me. I've never been very fortunate. But what about Lieutenant Lukáš, your honour?

JUDGE: The official battalion history does not report. Go home, Mr Švejk. Take my advice and go home.

ŠVEJK: But I said I'd look out for him.

JUDGE: It's over, Mr Švejk. The circle is broken once and for all.

The JUDGE leaves. Palivec's bar is revealed. MRS PALIVEC stands behind the bar. The VIRGIN MARY sits at the other table.

ŠVEJK: Any sign today, Mrs Palivec? I was held up.

MRS PALIVEC shakes her head.

TIME: Tick-tock.

ŠVEJK: Well, one Velkopopovický while I'm waiting then, Mrs Palivec.

MRS PALIVEC: One Velkopopovický.

TIME: Tick-tock.

ŠVEJK: He'll be along soon. Lieutenant Lukáš is very punctual. He's a good officer. He should have been promoted long ago, but fortune never seemed to smile on him.

TIME: Tick-tock.

ŠVEJK: Did you have anyone in the war, holy mother?

VIRGIN MARY does not respond.

TIME: Tick-tock.

ŠVEJK: I'll just wait a little longer. They'll be here. Vodička too. He's sure to be here. He's too smart to have got mixed up in that racket. You know, it reminds me of a time I was waiting for Ferdinand – that's Ferdinand the dog shit collector, not Ferdinand the chemist – He was to be there at six –

TIME: Ding. Ding. Ding. Ding. Ding. Ding... Ding.

The sound of dogs barking rises. The light fades as ŠVEJK proceeds with his story.

The End.